THE ADVENTURES OF ELT THE SUPER DOG
TROUBLE ON TRIANTHIUS

DANIEL R. PARD

authorHOUSE®

AuthorHouse™
1663 Liberty Drive
Bloomington, IN 47403
www.authorhouse.com
Phone: 1 (800) 839-8640

This is a work of fiction. All of the characters, names, incidents, organizations, and dialogue in this novel are either the products of the author's imagination or are used fictitiously.

Published by AuthorHouse 12/10/2015

ISBN: 978-1-5049-6656-6 (sc)
ISBN: 978-1-5049-6655-9 (hc)
ISBN: 978-1-5049-6657-3 (e)

Library of Congress Control Number: 2015920074

Print information available on the last page.

# ACKNOWLEDGMENTS

I wish to thank Brad Pard for the map art as well as Elt's website design on eltsadventures.com. Once again, a very special thank you to Heidi Lockridge, for her patience and supreme editing talents in perfecting the novel's presentation.

Ralph's Neighborhood

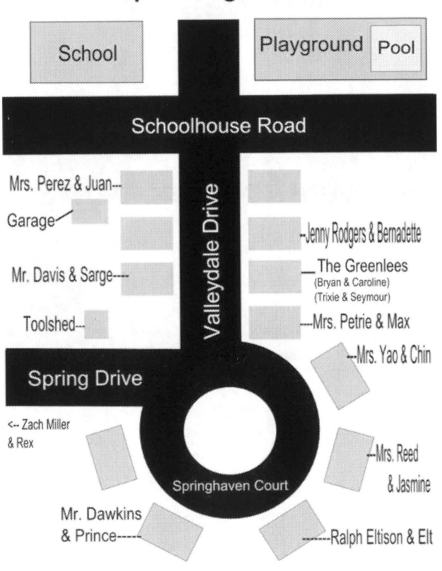

Downtown Spring Valley

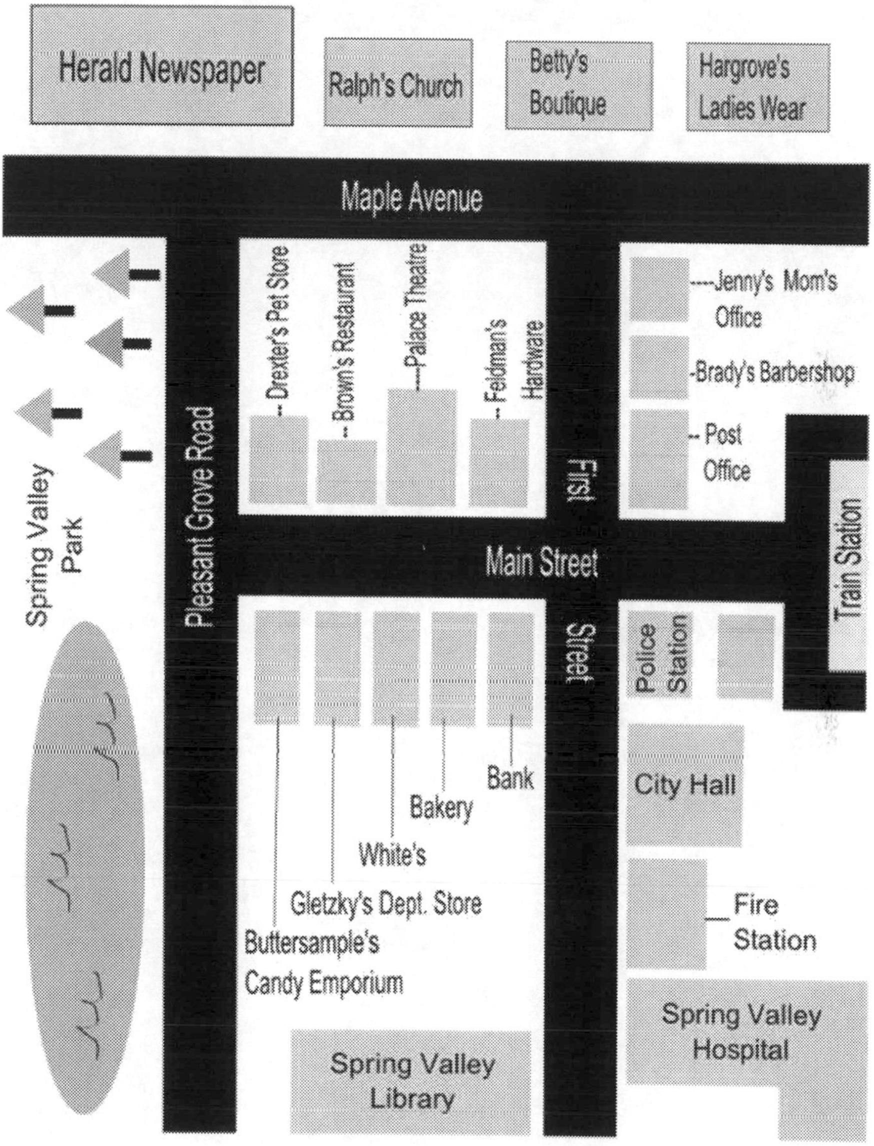

Herald Newspaper

Ralph's Church

Betty's Boutique

Hargrove's Ladies Wear

Maple Avenue

Spring Valley Park

Pleasant Grove Road

Drexter's Pet Store

Brown's Restaurant

Palace Theatre

Feldman's Hardware

Jenny's Mom's Office

Brady's Barbershop

Post Office

First Street

Train Station

Main Street

Police Station

City Hall

Bank

Bakery

White's

Gletzky's Dept. Store

Buttersample's Candy Emporium

Fire Station

Spring Valley Hospital

Spring Valley Library

DEDICATION

Thank you Mom for your never ending love and support. I am certain that you and Dad are reading this one together…..

CHAPTER 1

"WE'VE GOT THIS," THOUGHT THE retriever as he gazed out at the open waters. The summer's late day sun shimmered against the vast, restless waters of the San Francisco Bay. Seated confidently beside his human, twelve year-old Amy Pendergrass, Sparky, the heroic space traveling Golden Retriever, studied the waves as his human scrunched her toes into the sandy beach.

With her junior surfboard in hand, Amy cautiously scanned the scene before her. The riptides were one danger; the Great White Sharks on the prowl, another. She was careful, but not afraid. Amy's father had been a professional surfer in his earlier days, and through years of training with him, Amy had become a prolific surfer for her age. From time to time, she still ventured out with him and witnessed his superb techniques. One day, Amy hoped to be on the professional tour, traveling to far-away destinations with only one goal in mind; to be the best surfer in the world.

There were no waves too immense for this young adventurer. Her canine owned a similar mindset, as the retriever too, was an avid surfer.

Sparky always accompanied his human to the beach. Not only did Sparky surf alongside Amy, but late at night, while Amy was asleep, the super dog would sharpen his prolific skills on the waves. Part of his success was due to the spectacular stone secretly attached to the inside of his collar. Another factor was Sparky's amazing ability to remain balanced on the board.

Great White Sharks were prevalent in the San Francisco Bay. Scores of area surfers were well aware of the dangers of shark attacks. Sparky too was "in tune" with the dangers of the "beasts of the bay." There was one particular shark that was aware of the surfing canine. Sparky referred to his adversary as "Old Blue." The Great White frequented a certain area of the bay, both day and night.

Although the predator held a distinct advantage in the water, Sparky's ability to fly aided in his prompt escape. But he didn't stop there. His supreme strength allowed him to initiate a counter-attack. A couple of swift blows to the snout sent "Old Blue" splattering away.

"The waves look a little tricky today Sparky," observed Amy. She expected a response from her trusted canine. Sparky belted out a few crisp yelps. With a rope draped around his neck connected to his own surfboard balanced on his back, he lunged toward the waiting waters. Amy smiled at Sparky and dashed off toward the waves. Sparky softened his pace and followed Amy closely, for he could have easily outrun his human.

The girl and her companion leaped into the oncoming waves, disappearing into the vast effervescence of their salty surroundings. Amy climbed onto her board, her balance not affected by the bay's wicked tremors. Sparky's transition from swimming to boarding was equally impressive. The two battled the high tide victoriously for nearly an hour before hanging up their boards for the afternoon.

After conquering the best the beach had to offer them that day, Amy dried off while Sparky shook all the salty water off of his golden, shiny coat. "I think I'll have enough money to buy two cheeseburgers today," announced Amy. She smiled at Sparky, and then bent down to share a hug with him.

Sparky gleefully wagged his tail, for he was familiar with the word "cheeseburger." It was his favorite human food. As they sat enjoying their delicacy on a picnic bench along the beach, Sparky heard a low, distinct garble emanating from the stone under his collar. It was a low drone, undetected by Amy, and drowned by the pounding of the waves and screeches of the seagulls. Did the salt water somehow damage the stone? Sparky knew that was highly unlikely, for he was an avid swimmer, and the water had never affected the stone in that manner before. But was the noise a transmission and if so, from whom?

As Amy and Sparky walked home, the Golden Retriever listened carefully for any more noises, but there was nothing. He carried on with the rest of his day. There was his dogfood dinner, for the burger was only a late day snack. Playing "catch" in the yard with a miniature football followed. Sparky had to tone down his leaping ability, for he could have easily flown to wherever the ball was thrown. The final event of the day was a ten minute grooming. Amy possessed a unique talent of preventing those annoying knots in Sparky's fur.

While Amy showered, Sparky dutifully combed the backyard, only stopping for a few seconds to take care of business. Amy's property wasn't vast, but large enough to provide plenty of exercise room for the retriever and Amy.

Now the story behind Sparky's unique talents was very similar to Elt's story, but to a much larger degree. San Francisco was a massive American city, definitely not "Small Town USA" like Spring Valley, and California was a very sizeable state, one of the biggest in America. Being chosen to protect the human race, as well as every other race of beings on Earth in and around San Francisco, was a monumental honor.

Trianthians first discovered California as early as the gold rush days of the late 1800s. Yes, Trianthians were aiding civilizations way before Coladeus's time. Sparky's claim to fame, as he boastfully related to Elt when they first met, was the total salvation of California. Unbeknownst to Amy, her mom and dad, and the rest of the human race, Sparky and the Trianthians mended a sizeable crack in the San Andreas Fault. Without their covert assistance, in the middle of one night two summers ago, the Golden State would possess an island of its own. The scientists involved with the crisis held no answers to how the fault line mended itself so quickly.

Sparky was chosen by Coladeus and his team, in the same fashion as his fellow canine and friend from Spring Valley. He was young, intelligent, strong, and eager. Amy, like Ralph Eltison, walked her young retriever one day. Little did she realize that she was being watched by Matheun, from miles and miles deep into outer space. The clincher for the Trianthians was the canine's unique surfing talent.

Sparky's family had installed a doggie door just weeks before Coladeus arrived late one night to greet the candidate retriever. While taking care of business one late night, Sparky was confronted by the Trianthian. Somehow, in the same manner Elt was confronted years later, Sparky never barked, for although there was a stranger in the field behind his yard, in an egg-shaped whatever, Coladeus radiated a calming effect that soothed him. The Trianthian explained his purpose there, applied the stone to the back of Sparky's collar, and informed the canine that he would be contacted in two Earth days. By that time, all of Sparky's newly discovered super powers would be intact. The rest was history.

Now ever since Sparky had beamed back down to Earth after the mission to Titan, he had heard nothing concerning the whereabouts of the Trianthians or their evil enemies, the Quadrasones. Sparky wasn't even aware that Coladeus and his crew had catapulted twenty-five years into the future, assisting Elt and the time travelers.

Now this evening, all was tranquil. Amy had fallen asleep in bed while reading a surfing novel. Her mom and dad were watching television, and Sparky rested at the foot of Amy's bed. His eyes were closing, for he too was exhausted. Even as a dog with super powers, surfing always tuckered him out; plus a cheeseburger in his belly may have been another factor.

The canine began to dream. He was flying over the San Andreas Fault, Coladeus at his side in some sort of a one-person flying mechanism. The Earth was shaking; the fault line was tearing apart. Both Sparky and Coladeus noticed another flying machine ahead of them, spitting out rays of energy at the cracks in the ground. The rays seemed to be doing more harm than good. Sparky didn't know what was occurring, but it seemed like Coladeus was well aware of who was in the other apparatus.

"Who is that?" barked Sparky. Coladeus didn't answer. Wisps of clouds began to screen the dog and the Trianthian, and whoever it was in front of them disappeared in the clouds. Sparky began to snap out of his dream.

Suddenly, there was a disturbance; possibly not loud enough to wake a slumbering human, but easily enough to arouse a half-groggy canine. The sound was sort of a bird-like screech, but other than owls, there were no usual bird sounds at night, especially a screech like that. Certainly there were no snallygasters about; the legends of those creatures came only from the east coast. The screeching stopped suddenly; then there was a thud. Sparky leaped off the bed and darted downstairs.

"That dang raccoon, rummaging through our garbage cans again," whispered Sparky to himself as he swooped through his doggie door. He plowed straight for the garbage cans but then halted in his tracks. The cans were upright and intact; the lids tightly secured.

There were no other sounds, but something was definitely not right. He could feel it. The hairs on Sparky's back began to rise.

Beyond Sparky's backyard, a stretch of woods and a nominal clearing lay before reaching the neighbors' backyards. No one in the neighborhood was quite sure who owned the property. It was too small to erect another house; it was more like a buffer zone between residences. As Sparky approached the woods, he noticed a faint light flashing on and off, on and off. And there was a hissing noise, like steam out of an over-heated car radiator.

With ease, Sparky leaped over his fence and cautiously strode through the wooded area. He crept slowly through the brush, the hissing noise becoming louder as he approached the source of the disturbance. Sparky was less than fifty feet away from whatever was out there.

Sparky resisted the urge to bark, for he wanted to know what was out there before he warned anyone else in the neighborhood. He kept low and crept closer to the site. Sparky couldn't detect anyone, no one following him or in hiding. Nestled in a small clearing, between a copse of evergreens, sat some sort of alien spacecraft, but what kind? It wasn't Trianthian egg-shaped, but resembled more of a saucer shape, more like what one would see in a UFO movie.

Daniel R. Pard

A growl erupted from his throat, the hairs on his back up a full ninety degrees. He heard a clanging noise, and the door to the alien ship slid slowly open. A strange mist and dark green light appeared as a creature exited. It only took a few seconds for Sparky to recognize the visitor from another world. The hairs on his back eased, but he remained cautious. "You," muttered Sparky. "What are you doing here?"

CHAPTER 2

MATHEUN FELT THE FAMILIAR TINGLING sensation permeate his body as he transported back to Trianthius I, twenty-five years into the future. When he realized that he was indeed back on his ship, the scene before him was befuddling.

Only seconds ago, the Trianthian first officer was in Spring Valley, twenty-five years into the future. Edward Livingstone had just transported himself to an unknown destination. It was time for the alien to head back. It was time for Ralph, Elt, and the rest of the time travelers to head back to present day Spring Valley. The first officer opened his eyes.

"We're under attack!" shouted a fellow Trianthian in their native dialect. Matheun sprinted out of his module and didn't halt until he was secured in the elevator, heading for the bridge. He could feel the ship's vibrations as it maneuvered past some unforeseen foe.

Just a short time ago, Trianthius I had zoomed faster than it had ever raced, spinning endless revolutions around Earth. Although Mogulus, the most brilliant of the Trianthian scientists had calculated the exact formula for the Trianthians to travel into the future, he wasn't quite sure how the trip would affect the overall stability of the Trianthian vessel. And now it was under some sort of attack!

The bridge elevator door swooshed open. The first officer hustled past a couple of shipmates and leaped into his station. He slapped a few buttons and stared at his scanner. So engrossed was he in the moment, Matheun never acknowledged his captain's presence, but he knew he was there.

"Sir, our scanners indicate that there are twelve enemy fighters pursuing Trianthius I," reported Matheun in a tense Trianthian dialect. "I'm researching their origin now."

"No need to proceed with that directive," instructed Coladeus. The captain sat quietly in his chair, his illuminating glow diminished even more since the last time Matheun had seen him.

During the barrage of incoming enemy forces outside of Earth, Coladeus had waited patiently for his first officer to return. During that spell, Trianthius I had sustained significant damages to its defense shields. A counter attack could have been accomplished with the very powerful defense system, Litoses, on board Trianthius I. Litoses could launch rays that were fueled by Trianthian crystals from the ship's lower section. But the use of Litoses would certainly have drained Trianthius I of almost all of its energy, making a trip back to the present impossible.

The Earth strike force consisted of one and two- defender fighters, sleek and potent. The force didn't require a mother ship, for the planes departed from an air force base on Earth. The fighter jets resembled F15 fighters, but they were faster and maneuvered the outer layers of Earth's atmosphere with great agility. The planes were equipped with laser technology, but it was inferior to Litoses.

Trianthius I began to shake wildly, and then stabilized as it outraced its pursuers. The ship was maintaining a safe distance between itself and the enemy fighters. "Evidently, the humans have developed an aggressive space surveillance system in the last twenty-five years," observed Coladeus.

"Shall we defend ourselves?" asked Matheun.

"Negative. We need enough fuel to get back to present duracep time. Please set the coordinates for our return."

Matheun selected a few switches and buttons. "Coordinates set," he announced. A Trianthian officer near Matheun signaled to him. Matheun carefully examined the readings on his screen and then addressed the captain. "The earthlings are attempting to communicate with us. Shall I send a response?"

"That will not be necessary," returned Coladeus. "Initiate sequence." Trianthius I responded.

The Earth squadron closed in on the spaceship, but Trianthius I surprised the humans by turning around and heading straight for them. Caught off guard, the flying squadron's wall of defense broke into panicked pieces and dispersed in haphazard directions. Trianthius I increased its speed, breaking away from their pursuers. The ship sped towards Earth, but then changed direction so it would remain safely away from the planet's atmosphere. By the time the fighter jets were able to recover from the Trianthian maneuver and assemble themselves back into attack formation, the Trianthian vessel was gone.

The Trianthian ship now began its relentless run of reverse revolutions around the planet. Coladeus watched intensely as the ship's speed increased. Did they pass the enemy squadron as they circled around Earth? No one knew.

The trip only lasted about one earth minute, but it seemed like an eternity for Coladeus and his crew. Something troubling was happening to the Trianthians. Their green, vibrant glow, their energy source, was fading. They were struggling, listless. In the last day or so, the crew had endured two stressful voyages at very intense speeds. Trianthius I began slowing to normal speed with Earth in its background.

Meanwhile, the Earth squadron was bewildered. They had attempted communication with the unidentified vessel, but received no response. Next, they were in hot pursuit, but only firing to prevent the UFO from entering Earth's atmosphere. Then, in a flash, the spacecraft had turned, disrupted their alignment, and then it had sped away and vanished. Certainly, even in the future, Earth had not witnessed a spaceship that could travel close to the speed of light. It was unfathomable!

"Can anyone give me a location on the target?" asked one of the fighter pilots.

"Negative," said another pilot, followed by more of the same responses.

The squadron broke off into different sectors and patrolled the area for about a half-hour before heading back to base for re-fueling. The unidentified vessel was gone, never to be seen again.

CHAPTER 3

"LET'S SEE IF WE CAN obtain a more precise picture here," said the determined professor. He peered through the telescope and adjusted a number of dials before he was able to view a clearer picture of the August night sky. Professor Stanley Greenlee had made himself famous with his time travel discoveries. He had just returned from a week-long holiday following the wildly successful but extremely unpredictable public demonstration of an excursion into the future.

Ever since his return, the professor's priorities had changed, when it came to science, that is. For his entire life, Stanley had focused on time travel. He had been caught-up in all the hoopla and excitement over the time machine and its effect on the science world. But somewhere in the back of his mind, through the voyage into Spring Valley's future, the explosive return to the laboratory, and all the events that followed, Stanley began to recall some things that later were just too hard to explain. The one image that kept returning was that of the alien he met during the voyage. With that image in the recesses of his memory, the subject of alien presence and life on other planets superseded all of the professor's goals and objectives. Time travel was no longer his top priority.

There were other bits of recollections regarding the astonishing return to present time in Spring Valley that day. There were specs involving his children's friend Ralph. Then there was something about Ralph's dog, Elt, along with several other neighborhood pets. How in the world did Ralph, all the animals, and a glowing green man venture to the future Spring Valley without a time machine? And how did they rescue him, his kids, and Henry Buttersample, in just a number of hours?

Professors Greenlee and Van Hausen discussed Stanley's unbelievable recollections. They both agreed that since neither of them witnessed Ralph and the pets near the time machine or the laboratory during the time of the explosion, that Greenlee had somehow created these memories subconsciously during the stressful return to Spring Valley. Bryan and Caroline Greenlee never mentioned a word about what they remembered.

So upon his return, Professor Greenlee concentrated his efforts on the restoration of the space labs and observatory tower. Van Hausen was in charge of the clean up and re-building of his main lab which was devastated by the time machine's blast. Construction crews were hired to repair the hole in the roof and to remove all the debris. Luckily, the time machine's rotating landing pad was salvageable, not totally devastated by the explosion.

So while Van Hausen attended to the laboratory, Greenlee and a select few associates began restoring the space-related equipment on campus. Number one on the list was their observatory. Stretched half-way across the campus, nestled on top of the highest available peak, stood the three story brick structure that resembled a barn silo.

The observatory housed a magnificent telescope, enabling researchers and enthusiasts to view planetary systems, stars, comets, and eclipses. The "observatory tower," as it was named, was constructed in the late nineteen seventies, for Professor Van Hausen required a device to lure researchers and scientists to his fairly new complex. He conducted astronomy seminars, especialy when UFOs were the "big story" in the news circa 1978.

Although Van Hausen was serious about space exploration and the use of the observatory tower, the time machine still stood in the forefront of all of his objectives. Through the years, the observatory tower, along with all of the satellite dishes and equipment pertaining to space research, took a backseat and were not maintained well. This was too bad for had the equipment been given proper attention, someone may have observed a few outer space visits from the Trianthians.

Magnus I, as it was named previously by Professor Van Hausen, was an extremely large telescope that was capable of studying distant stars and planets. In today's time, a telescope of this magnitude would have cost millions of dollars. Funds generated by the time machine excursion enabled Van Hausen and Greenlee to upgrade the telescope and restore it to functionability.

"Let's see if we can get a clearer picture of Jupiter," instructed Greenlee. The professor peered through the giant telescope. He backed away, so his assistant, Amanda Walker, could gaze into the telescope.

"That's amazing," breathed Amanda as she soaked in the beauty and majesty of the solar system's largest planet. "Do you think we'll ever travel to planets like Jupiter?" Little did she know that there had already been a voyage, one to Saturn to be exact.

The professor smiled and gazed at his watch. "We traveled through time. I'm sure we'll make it to Jupiter one day. But for now, we need to wrap this up for the evening, so I can make it home. I could watch the events up there all night if given the chance."

"Yes Professor," grinned Amanda.

So the professor and Amanda retired for the evening. There was still work to do, mostly cleaning, but that could be accomplished another day. It was now Professor Greenlee's goal to make sure the observatory was in full operation by the fall, so that on every starry occasion, discoveries could be made by the students and faculty.

Somewhere out there, in the far extremities of his memories, there was an alien, the boy down the street, and the neighborhood pets. Somehow those memories were there for a reason. But for now, the main focus was restoring the observatory. Little did Professor Greenlee know that his telescope would play an intricate part in the coming events, both on Earth and in Spring Valley. Visitors from another world were coming, some were going to be friendly, the others, not so friendly.

CHAPTER 4

THE DARK, OMNIPOTENT CREATURE STOOD outside the spacecraft and stared at the Golden Retriever. There was an eerie silence for a few seconds, each being waiting the other out, to see who was going to make the first move. The only alien that had ever visited him was Coladeus, and this definitely wasn't Coladeus, or any Trianthian for that matter.

The creature's eyes glowed slightly as it continued to stare down at Sparky. Steam continued to flow out of posterior of the saucer-shaped ship. Sparky drew closer. He didn't look the creature eye-to-eye, for although he knew the alien, he still didn't trust those eyes. The alien was a stranger to Earth, but not to Sparky. Klecktonis, the triangular-headed alien with laser-beam eyes, maintained her position just outside of her ship.

Coladeus had never mentioned where space heroes like Klecktonis, Myotaur, and Widenmauer had originated, but Sparky figured that they were very close. Since he and Elt were the last to board and the first to depart from the mission to Titan, perhaps a planet like Venus or Mars was the home of one of the creatures on their team.

"What's going on dudette?" asked Sparky softly. Of course, she didn't understand his canine language. Klecktonis stood firmly, her hands resting on her hips, or the body part that resembled her hips. She gazed back at her ship, and then muttered a repetitive chirp, much like a bird warning other birds when there was danger. Her eyes began to intensify, but then softened.

Within seconds, a second creature emerged from the ship. Sparky knew exactly who it was; his Sorgian replicate. Coladeus had always referred to this Sorgian as "Ratar." Sparky always referred to him as "Rat," with no defamation of the Sorgian's name intended.

Although there was no formal communication, Sparky understood why Klecktonis and Rat were there. A mission was in the works, and it somehow involved him. A plan was in motion and Klecktonis was there to escort him, with Rat staying behind to replicate the Golden Retriever.

Sparky prepared himself for the transformation, although he was quite unsure if Klecktonis could pull it off. Coladeus had always performed the replication in the past. Now it was time for Sparky to trust his fellow space hero.

The Golden Retriever edged closer to Klecktonis and the Sorgian. The alien reached into a satchel she had strapped around her mid-waist and grabbed the replicating device. It resembled the unit used by the Trianthian leader in previous missions. She knew she had to be quick, for she wasn't interested in meeting with any humans that evening.

"How did you get one of those cool toys?" inquired Sparky softly. Once again, the alien didn't quite understand what he was muttering about, but continued with the replication process. Klecktonis first weaved the device around Sparky's contours, and then shifted her attention to Ratar. In less than a minute, Sparky was face-to-face with his twin.

"All right Rat, you know the drill," instructed Sparky. "Take care of my Amy." The new Sparky yelped, shook himself, and then darted off to Sparky's house. The retriever shook his head. "I wonder why my humans don't know it's me?" He shrugged his upper torso and stepped into the spaceship. Klecktonis scanned the area briefly, and then joined Sparky inside. The spaceship door closed.

Once inside, the canine followed the alien up to the ship's version of the cockpit. The ship was about twice the size of the Trianthian space pod, but was way smaller than Trianthius I. It consisted of two levels. A sequestered area upstairs housed two chairs, one for the pilot, a second for a co-pilot, but in Sparky's case, a passenger seat.

Sounding more like a rusty clunker from an old junkyard, Klecktonis's ship blasted into the night sky. Sparky stared at The Golden Gate Bridge in the distance through the narrow windows in front of him. If folks in the neighborhood heard the ruckus, by the time they reached their front porch, the ship and it's clunky engine were long gone.

To call the spaceship a "hunk of junk" would have been rude, especially to someone who could melt another's face off with her laser beam eyes. And although the spaceship rattled and shrilled, it did manage to pack a powerful punch. Fueled by vegetation and certain oils shaved from rocks on her home planet, the flying craft held fuel reserves in a tank located near the bottom. So there they were… two heroes on their way to rescue their mentor and friend.

The saucer-shaped vessel remained low, just above the mountain ranges and below the higher drifting clouds. There were no lights on the ship, so no one could see anything flying by them or above them. Radar systems would have difficulty detecting craft flying that low. The only drawback was the sound. Folks may not have been able to see, but they definitely could have heard that peculiar noise above them.

Sparky and Klecktonis were in for a rocky ride, for the late evening winds were just enough of a factor to keep the ship shifting from side to side. "It's like riding the waves without the water," thought Sparky as he maintained a certain "coolness" throughout the voyage. Klecktonis struggled to stay on course as the ship darted and dashed from right to left, and then right again. Where was she heading? Why wasn't she venturing out to space? What was her plan? How had she found him? And how did the Sorgian end up with her? These questions were whirling through the canine's mind.

Although the trip seemed perilous, Sparky was confident that the alien knew what she was doing. He was unaware, for one, that she was even capable of piloting an aircraft. The ship slithered across the mountains, barely passing by its tip-tops. Sparky lost all track of time as the vessel trekked over the rugged terrain.

Klecktonis reached above and selected a number of buttons on a console. A picture appeared on a small, overhead screen located next to the console. Sparky recognized the image, for it was Elt, his friend, his comrade. "We're going to pick up Elt?" questioned Sparky eagerly, but Klecktonis gave him no answer. She continued to guide her ship under a patch of low-lying clouds.

All of a sudden, through the turmoil of the treacherous trip, Sparky felt an uneasiness settle around him, another presence in the room. He picked up the scent, it was a familiar one, but not an exact scent. Sparky twisted in his seat. "Who's hiding back there?" he challenged. "Come out before I have to drag you out."

After a few seconds, the stranger surged out of hiding, climbing out from behind a stretch of conduit-like material that led to the ship's engines below. Through the vast darkness in that area of the cabin, all Sparky could see was a set of big white eyes. Klecktonis turned around, motioned for the stranger to reveal himself, and then continued to steer the ship. Now Sparky knew who it was.

"Come on Dude, join the experience," encouraged the Golden Retriever. The being moved slowly, against the swerving of the ship, and then steadied himself in front of his shipmates. He didn't utter a word; he just stood still and stared directly at Sparky. "You must be Elt's Sorgian," said Sparky. "Oleo, isn't it? Clever, very clever," commented Sparky. He motioned to Klecktonis. "So, did Coladeus set this...?"

A beeping sound interrupted Sparky's inquiry. Multi-colored lights flashed across the console in front of the alien. "What's going on laser eyes?" quipped Sparky. "What's all the excitement about?"

What Sparky didn't realize was that they were close to their destination...Elt. Klecktonis reached for a radio-like device below the main control panel and initiated the power. A scratchy, fuzzy noise emanated from the device, barely audible over the noises caused by the vibrations of the ship.

"Where are we going after we snatch Elt?" asked Sparky. "I need answers." Klecktonis turned around and spoke to Sparky for the first time. There was no need for a distransulator or decoder, for she only stated one word; a word that carried the same definition in all languages of all species.

"Quadrasones."

A chill slivered down Sparky's spine. He knew now where they were headed. He knew who was in trouble. Sparky drew closer to the radio device. Klecktonis pointed to where Sparky needed to activate the speaker.

"Elt, Elt, can you read me? Sparky hesitated, and then spoke again. "Dude, this is Sparky."

Within seconds, Sparky heard faintly, "I can read you Sparky."

There was static interfering with their communications for a brief moment, but then Sparky continued. "There's trouble on Trianthius! Coladeus needs us! Dude, we're on our way to pick you up."

CHAPTER 5

"DO YOU SEE ANYTHING?" ASKED the Cocker Spaniel.

"Not yet," returned the super dog.

Situated just outside her front gate, Bernadette and Elt both stared at the night sky. Every imaginable star and planet could be viewed, for there wasn't a cloud in the sky. The canines weren't exactly sure what they were searching for. Elt remembered the egg-shaped Trianthian pod, and both he and Bernadette definitely recalled the appearing and disappearing via the transport modules. But how was Sparky going to pick up Elt? Surely Sparky didn't own a space vehicle or human flying machine. Elt wondered what was going on. What was happening on Trianthius? Had Coladeus and the Trianthians ever been able to return to the present after rescuing Elt and his friends in the time travel mission?

Scores of questions continued to flow through both Elt's and Bernadette's minds. A strange yet exciting feeling overcame them both as they anxiously anticipated contact with Elt's friend Sparky. Would there be lights, sounds, or flashes? The pod cast only a shadow; would they even be able to see whatever Sparky was flying in?

Within seconds, Elt's and Bernadette's keen sense of hearing detected an unfamiliar sound. It was heading their way. "I hear something," alerted Elt.

"Me too," added Bernadette.

The sputtering ship approached. Luckily, the noise was not loud enough to wake a human from his or her sleep, for it was night, and it was late. Canines, however, easily heard the disturbance. Elt and Bernadette watched as the black shadow soared past them and headed straight for Elt's yard.

"It's headed for my human's house," warned Elt. "Let's go!" The two dogs dashed towards the Eltison house. Elt wanted to slow down, so Bernadette could keep up. But Elt was way too excited and abandoned Bernadette in a flash. She understood, for Elt was deeply concerned. Sparky, his friend, was most likely in that ship. In addition, that ship just flew too close for comfort over his home while his humans were fast asleep.

Behind Ralph's house, just beyond the backyard fence, stretched a patch of woods. It was larger than the woods behind Sparky's house, but there was no field to land in, just trees. The vessel cruised over the fence and crashed into some trees in the woods. This ruckus did stir up some of the neighborhood guardians. Chin, the ever-diligent Chow-Chow, heard the screeching noise, and watched as the ship whizzed over his house. He yelped a series of warning barks, but the rest of the neighborhood dogs were inside. Jasmine was asleep on her porch when the excitement occurred. She opened her eyes as Elt zoomed past her house, followed seconds later by Bernadette.

Jasmine sprang off the porch and trailed them to Elt's backyard, then stopped and stood beside the Cocker Spaniel who was looking ahead at Elt. About twenty yards ahead of them, with his two front paws resting near the top of the fence, Elt sniffed the woods in front of him, contemplating his next move.

"What do you think it is?" whispered Bernadette.

Jasmine nodded her head. "Something weird. Maybe something not from our world." The girls edged closer to Elt. He turned around to acknowledge their presence.

"It has to be Sparky," stated Elt. "But I'm not sure. I'm trying to catch a scent of him." He continued to sniff the area.

"I'm ready if you are," proposed Jasmine. It was pitch black in the woods. The wan evening light over the yard spoke of the last remnants of summer. Even the remaining fireflies that had brilliantly lit the night sky in early summer now only created a weak twinkling.

Suddenly, in the distance, about fifty yards away, the three pets sensed a presence. Something was definitely out there. They knew that a move had to be made.

"You think it's that alien guy?" asked Jasmine.

Elt shook his head. "It's not Matheun. It's something else." Jasmine and Bernadette began taking whiffs, attempting to help their friend. "Let's go find out," charged Elt. He eased back a couple of steps, and then effortlessly soared over the backyard fence. Jasmine scaled the fence and joined her friend.

"Wait for me! How am I going to get over?" inquired Bernadette. Elt knew that he could have easily jumped the fence with Bernadette strapped to his back, but he had other plans for her.

"You stay here," instructed Elt. "Just in case we need help."

"What? But it's kind of creepy out here," whimpered Bernadette. "I'm not used to your yard. It sounds different and it smells weird." Elt confronted Bernadette; their noses touching through the fence holes.

"We won't be far away." He spoke reassuringly. "Bark if you need us, but not too loud." Bernadette nodded. She wasn't too thrilled about Elt's decision, but she understood his reasoning.

Elt had never really explored the woods behind the backyard. This was definitely going to be new territory for him and Jasmine. The tabby had wandered through the area before, but it had been quite some time ago, so her memory of the terrain was vague. Now they both had to discover what was out there, and quickly. Elt's friend could be hurt, or in trouble.

The two turned away carefully, plodded through the twigs and pine needles, and waded through the briars, attempting to create as little sound as possible. Elt could have flown, but there were too many trees. Plus, he required some room for take-off.

The sporadic, twinkling light provided by the scattered fireflies, along with the rhythmic drones of the bullfrogs, crickets, and katydids, provided enough cover for Elt and Jasmine to weave their way through the thicket before arriving at their destination. Elt remembered the Trianthian pod, especially its shape in the nightly shadows. This was no pod. Its shape was haunting, yet something about it seemed non-threatening. One thing was for sure….Elt didn't sense a Trianthian on board.

Steam emerged from the object, in all different directions. Both the canine and feline heard movement inside; their ears perked and their heads shifted to one side, attempting to determine what was in there and if it was friendly.

Suddenly, an opening formed at the top of the vessel and an eerie source of light emerged. The first being appeared, its shadow undetectable due to the uneven outlay of light. Jasmine and Elt remained hidden in the brush, ready to defend themselves if any undesirable fiend became aggressive and attacked. The being coughed as he exited. "Where in your world did you learn how to drive?" winced the being. Elt breathed a sigh of relief. He understood exactly what the stranger was saying, for it was canine speak. He couldn't contain himself.

"Sparky!" Elt's stage whisper was loud enough for the retriever to hear above the wood's serenade of insects and reptiles. Sparky turned his head in Elt's direction.

"Yes, it's me, Dude, didn't you receive my message?"

"Uh, I guess we did," beamed Elt.

"Then….righteous dude, it's time for a paw bump." Sparky held up his right paw. Elt moved toward him to return the bump but Sparky's eyes suddenly widened. He leaped toward Elt and shouted, "Kitty cat at ten o'clock!" Surprised, Elt was still able to block his path and protect the startled Jasmine who jumped onto Elt's back in fear. Her claws dug deeply into the super dog's coat.

"Yow, Jasmine! The claws!" winced Elt. "Dude, it's ok!" he continued. "She's with me. She's part of the team."

Sparky backed off and took a deep breath. He focused his attention on Jasmine. "Sorry there. These darn instincts, you know, get the best of me sometimes."

"No harm taken Fido," snickered Jasmine, trying to recover some of her pride. She jumped down from Elt.

"Did you fly this thing?" inquired Elt.

Sparky shook himself. "Oh no, I hitched a ride with ole Laser-Beam Eyes herself." Elt remembered Sparky uttering the words "Laser Eyes" before. But before Elt could remember who the retriever was referring to, she emerged from the ship. The triangular-headed silhouette could be easily distinguished, even in the darkness of night.

"This is *her* space transport machine?" asked Elt.

Sparky shook his head. "Have you ever flown on a human 'aeroplane'?" Elt and Jasmine both shook their heads no. "Well, I have," returned Sparky. "And let me tell you, this thing is nothing like it. In fact, it was horrific!"

Elt, Jasmine, and Sparky gazed upward and watched the intimidating figure from another planet, finish her climb out of her spaceship, thrust outward, and land on her feet in one lengthy, continuous motion. She stood straight in front of them; her eyes glowing softly. She spoke, but no one understood what she said.

"Dude, you should never catch a ride with a stranger," warned Sparky.

"But you *know* her….we know her," reasoned Elt.

"I don't want to know her that well," returned Sparky. "But deep down, I knew why she came for me. And that's why I'm here." Klecktonis strayed away from the group and began to inspect the ship's exterior, hoping to investigate any possible flaw in her vessel.

"I've never seen a pet, human, or even an alien that resembles something so off-the-wall scary," murmured Jasmine in disbelief.

"So where's Matheun? What's the mission? Are we going to help Coladeus?" inquired Elt as he continued to watch every move Klecktonis made.

"Helping Coladeus is the plan," remarked Sparky.

"So do we know where Coladeus and Mathuen are?" asked Elt.

"She knows." Sparky lifted his chin in Klecktonis's direction. "There's just one *problemo*. I've only understood one word from her this whole trip."

"What about your replicate?" asked Elt. "Isn't your human going to miss you?"

Sparky shook his head. "We got it covered brother." How he had managed to do that, no one even had time to ask him, for out from the ship appeared its last occupant. Elt recognized the being, while Jasmine sniffed with assurance, for she recalled the Sorgian's scent from the last time he visited Spring Valley. Oleo scrambled over to Elt, hugged him, and then hid himself under a magnolia bush.

"How did the Sorgians....?" questioned Elt.

"They knew something," guessed Sparky. "They must have had a plan." Klecktonis approached the group. She began to speak while pointing to various areas of the ship.

"What is she saying?" inquired Jasmine.

"I think she's telling us that her ship needs repairs," explained Elt.

"If we're traveling to Trianthius in this piece of junk, we're definitely going to need help," asserted Sparky.

Elt stared at both Klecktonis, and then the damaged ship. He was deep in thought.

"I know where we can get help," Elt responded. "From my human."

CHAPTER 6

TRIANTHIUS I EMERGED FROM A cloudy mist outside of Earth's atmosphere. After its multitudes of revolutions, Matheun regained himself enough to monitor his scanner.

Coladeus had fallen from his seat, further weakened by the strenuous trip. He struggled to rise. Two crew members rushed to his aide, but the captain graciously turned them away. He rose, and then returned to his seat.

"Do you have an accurate reading?" Coladeus asked roughly in his alien dialect.

Matheun turned and faced his captain. "Mogulus has never failed us, sir."

"We've returned to present day?" asked Coladeus.

Matheun nodded affirmatively.

"Any chance we were followed?" asked the Trainthian elder.

"Negative," returned the first officer after repeated scans of his screen. "Fuel levels are not optimal, yet they are sufficient enough to get us home."

"Excellent," exhaled Coladeus. "Then set your coordinates for Trianthius. Let's not be hasty, however, for we don't want to exhaust our fuel supply. We must retain enough power to maintain our defense shields."

"Should we establish communications?" questioned the first officer.

"Affirmative," replied Coladeus. "I have an uneasy feeling about what we'll encounter when we arrive at Trianthius."

Matheun selected a series of commands for his next directive. The fact that the glow in the room was only about half its normal brightness didn't affect the first officer's ability to carry out his commands. He and the entire crew, especially Coladeus, was suffering from a loss of strength. Matheun motioned for a crewmember. They conversed briefly.

"We have received no response from Trianthius, even on emergency broadcast channels," reported Matheun.

"Do we have acknowledgement that the transmission was received?"

"No sir."

Coladeus contemplated his next move. "Have we attempted transmissions to Trianthius II or Trianthius III?"

Trianthius did possess two other ships in their fleet; two were generally deployed at once, while one stayed in port, in case of a domestic situation, like an evacuation. Could one of these ships be battling an enemy?

A high percentage of Trianthian messages to one another were accomplished through transmission. Transmissions were silent exchanges, much like text messaging, but in code that only Trianthians could decipher. In rare emergency situations, the broadcast networks were used as well. Matheun tried to hail Trianthius II.

"No response from Trianthius II sir," he informed the captain. Then he hesitated, cocked his head and listened carefully, and then conferred with his fellow crewmember. "Sir, we have just received a transmission from Trianthius II, but it was garbled and illogical."

"What was their message?" asked the captain.

"There was interference, but I distinctly heard them say that the situation was normal, and no assistance was warranted at this time."

"I see," related Coladeus.

"But sir, I didn't offer assistance," commented Matheun.

"Exactly," deduced Coladeus. "It is my opinion that both Trianthius and our armada are under attack and rendered helpless."

"But they don't require our assistance?" inquired Matheun.

"I believe that was a warning," concluded Coladeus. "I feel that our suspicions are confirmed."

"You mean…?" asked Matheun.

Coladeus nodded and pressed his lips together. "Evidently, our planet and our forces have been subdued by the Quadrasones."

Everyone paused and looked up at the captain. No one spoke for a few moments. And then one of the crew members ventured a question. "But *how* sir? Our planetary shields are inpenetrable."

"The Quadrasones are an aggressive species," tutored Coladeus. "But also, a diligent one. They must have found a weakness, for we can all feel it." What Coladeus had stated was true and they all knew it. Their glow was diminished; their energy, low. "Somehow, they found a way" he continued. "We must gather all of our resources and plan a strategy for what we're about to encounter."

"Stay on course?" asked Matheun.

"Yes," affirmed Coladeus. "We must proceed with extreme caution."

"Yes sir."

Trianthius I forged ahead towards their home planet, not knowing what was in store for them. The unasked questions filled the cabin. Was Trianthius helpless? How would Trianthius I possess enough energy to get there and then confront the Quadrasones? Coladeus and his crew faced a possible trap by a formidable enemy. While the crew worked silently, they all knew the fate of their planet, their home, and their individual lives were at stake.

CHAPTER 7

A DULL, YELLOWISH HUE BARELY brightened an already gray, dingy room. The room's inhabitants scurried about in an ant-like fashion, obeying orders on the alien mothership. Although these beings were extra-terrestrials like the Trianthians, this particular species was different; not barbaric, but sinister. No one spoke, for they communicated through a telepathic mind-speak.

The leader was seated in his chair, which floated. In fact, the entire crew was stationed in levitating chairs, yet the rest of the equipment in the spacecraft was stationary. Their chairs moved about, from place to place.

The leader watched the scene before him intensely. His warship, close to two times the size of Trianthius I, hovered over its prey, its triumph. In front of him, projected upon his holographic view screen, stood Trianthius, its normally vibrant, green splendor diminished to lifeless, burnt yellow, as if it were an autumn leaf that had fallen to the ground, ready for its transformation into soil.

What kind of a monster would desire to destroy such a paradise as Trianthius? There was only one true enemy of the Trianthians, and the name of their leader was Zemak. There were countless mysteries surrounding the beings known as the Quadrasones. No one, not even the Trianthians, were aware of the Quadrasones' exact origin. They lived on no known planet. Had their planet been destroyed in ages past? Was that the reason the Quadrasones traveled like nomads, replenishing themselves before destroying their hosts?

What the Trianthians did know was that wherever they traveled, the Quadrasones weren't too far behind. Soon after Coladeus or one of his comrades led a successful excursion to aid a civilization, long after they were already on to the next mission, strange occurrences were reported. The planet involved was usually threatened. Sometimes the enemy was visible and other times it was unseen. There were instances where the Trianthians were forced to return, but when they arrived, the perpetrators were long gone. Fortunately, Earth had been spared a visit from this evil. Or had they?

Quadrasones possessed unique powers, all contained within their diamond-shaped heads. They communicated telepathically, across great distances, so there was no need for the species to possess mouths. Keen hearing and an incredible sense of smell were gifted attributes of this mysterious race, although their ears and nostrils were minute alongside their huge, white eyes.

Why the Quadrasones detested the Trianthians was another mystery. Mogulus, Coladeus, and other select elders had a theory; they thought that the diamond heads would prey upon a civilization recently aided by the Trianthians for one reason: the civilization was vulnerable. Over several duraceps, the friendly aliens figured out the Quadrasone tactic, and devised an action of their own to thwart the attacks.

The sighting on Titan was the first Quadrasone encounter in about three duraceps. Where had they been? What were they up to now? There was a reason for their disappearance, a very deadly one.

Zemak's haunting image reflected off the holograph before him. How he had relished this moment in time. Now he waited patiently for the last piece of the puzzle, the long-awaited prey to be swept into his web of destruction. He knew the end of the Trianthians simply relied on one factor, the capture and demise of Coladeus.

It was always Coladeus that had foiled his plans, his attacks. Although there was an obvious difference in ship size, the Trianthians had always outwitted their foes with clever strategies and more powerful weaponry. When he needed to use it, Coladeus outdueled Zemak with the litoses rays. The Quadrasones couldn't win for their laser technology was inferior. But now the tide had changed. The discovery had been made. The idea had flourished into reality, and they now owned the ultimate arsenal.

In the forefront of the lifeless planet, lie a still Trianthius II, floating uselessly in space just outside its planet's orbit. The super ship couldn't escape if it wanted to. Trianthius III was still quietly docked at its space port. The attack had occurred before there was a chance to deploy the last of the Trianthian fleet.

"Has there been a formal declaration of surrender from the Trianthian council?" transmitted Zemak to Dresant, his most trusted officer.

"No, Your Excellency."

Zemak had waited patiently, but his angst was beginning to get the better of him. He wanted to crush his nemesis now, not wonder if and when he would arrive. "Coladeus will come. When he does, we will be ready for him."

"Yes Excellency," returned Dresant.

CHAPTER 8

RALPH HAD FELT AFFECTION FROM his dog before, and in the middle of the night. The last time Elt had planted that many kisses on his favorite human, he had just returned home from his mission on Titan. Ralph giggled in his sleepy state. "Boy, what are you doing?" Elt paused for a moment, and then resumed his barrage of doggie kisses. Ralph opened his eyes. His dog stood above him, wagging his tail excitedly. As soon as Ralph rose out of bed, Elt leaped across the room, and enticed his human to follow him by darting in and out of the bedroom.

Inquisitively, Ralph tailed Elt out to the backyard. "Could Coladeus be visiting?" Ralph wondered. The boy was worried about the Trianthian. Was it possible that the extra- terrestrial had transported down to his backyard? Ralph knew that Coladeus wasn't feeling well the last time he saw his friend. Had the alien's condition improved?

"What are we doing out here boy?" asked Ralph. He could barely see where he was walking. It was difficult for Ralph to distinguish Elt's silhouette from the darkness of night. A faint light from the kitchen stove through the window enabled Ralph to elude obstacles in the yard. He stayed close to his canine.

"Wait a second boy." Ralph trotted back to the house, quietly entered the kitchen, and returned almost instantly with a functional flashlight. Elt began to trot over to the back fence. Ralph didn't know why Elt was veering back; he still saw no sign of Coladeus. What Ralph didn't expect were the visitors that accompanied Elt along the fenced area.

Before Elt had headed to Ralph's bedroom, Sparky and Jasmine had accompanied him to the backyard fence. Sparky was shocked to discover the gorgeous Cocker Spaniel on the other side.

"Who's the groovy chick?" asked Sparky.

"Uh, we're kind of like….," answered Elt.

Sparky smirked. "I get it."

Bernadette was excited to see her friends, and a bit surprised that she was about to meet a new one, but something was upsetting her. She settled down on the ground.

"Are you okay?" asked a concerned Elt. He bent down to nudge her.

"My tummy doesn't feel so good today," Bernadette had responded. "I'll nibble on some grass in your yard."

Now Elt sat down beside Bernadette, who slowly wagged her tail as Ralph shined the light at the two. Jasmine entered the scene next. Ralph followed her every move, casting the light into the tabby's direction. Jasmine fluttered past Elt and Bernadette, stopping in front of Sparky. The boy had no idea who that dog was. What in the world?

"Where did you come from?" inquired Ralph. He didn't sense any hostility on the part of the Golden Retriever. Elt walked over to Sparky and sat beside him. There were no growls or barks between the two canines.

Ralph bent down cautiously to pet the new dog. With the aid of the flashlight, Ralph noticed that the dog wore a collar. He continued petting the new dog, but stopped to examine the identification tag dangling from the collar.

"Sparky….your name is Sparky," discovered Ralph. He read further. "San Francisco, California?"

Sparky wagged his tail and licked Ralph's fingers. Ralph responded by rubbing behind his ears. The Golden Retriever sensed no harm from Elt's human. Then, for no other reason than to satisfy his own curiosity, Ralph twisted the canine's collar. And there it was: the same type of green stone that was affixed to his own dog's collar. "Whoa," Ralph spoke softly. Ralph inspected the stone for a few more seconds, and then let it go. Could it be? He figured Elt wasn't the only being on Earth granted powers by Coladeus, but what was this dog doing in his backyard in the middle of the night?

Sparky and Elt suddenly turned and vaulted over the fence with ease. Bernadette remained behind, watching them. Ralph pointed the flashlight in their direction. Whatever Elt and Sparky desired Ralph to see was beyond the fence. Ralph had only journeyed a handful of times in his young life to the wooded area behind his backyard; the main reason for jumping the barrier was to retrieve a baseball or football that had inadvertently made its way beyond the fence. Ralph's dad had made it clear that Ralph had to inform his father before he ever went exploring in those woods. He wasn't forbidden, but he was required to communicate with his father.

Only on one occasion, a couple of summers ago, had Ralph curiously scaled the fence and ventured into the "unknown." He pretended that he was an explorer, searching for gold in a forest filled with dinosaurs and other hostile predators. In reality, the only possible danger might have been a snake, or a rabid raccoon, although the chances for those encounters were minimal.

Ralph battled an imaginary fire-breathing dragon that guarded the gold at all costs. In reality, Ralph did end up with the treasure. He discovered an area in the woods filled with a selection of cool-looking stones that resembled gold. He also found a patch or two of poison ivy. It was an itchy situation to say the least.

Now a year had lapsed since Ralph had scaled the fence. It was pitch black outside. "What do I have to worry about?" whispered Ralph to himself. "I have two super dogs with me."

Elt and Sparky waited patiently while Ralph climbed over the fence. The boy was fortunate to be escorted by the two canines, for although he was close to home, the trip into darkness was not only scary, but difficult. Jasmine, in a last second decision, opted to join the join the boy and the two canines, leaving Bernadette behind in Ralph's yard.

Ralph could make out some flashing lights ahead of him, but the air was murky from the crash of the spaceship and so the scene was difficult to see clearly. What was it? He had experienced a plethora of bizarre encounters lately – aliens, deep space, and a time machine. What could be so bad?

Sparky, Elt, and Ralph slowed down and stopped about ten feet in front of the spaceship. Ralph's jaw dropped; he felt his heart skip a couple of beats. It was overwhelming. He had witnessed the arrival of Coladeus in his egg-shaped pod. He had traveled through time on a time machine. He had journeyed on board Trianthius I. But this was a real live alien spacecraft!

It became more mesmerizing, with a touch of terrifying on the side, when Ralph came face-to-face with the intimidating figure of Klecktonis. The alien peered at Ralph with her blazing, green eyes. He could see her silhouette, as ominous as it was, but it was those eyes that froze Ralph in his tracks. The boy was both mesmerized and frightened by the stranger's appearance. Who wouldn't be? She appeared to have three fingers, although it was difficult for Ralph to see. In one of her hands, the being held a tiny screen; about the size of a small book. She entered figures into the mini-computer. The boy and two canines continued to watch carefully every move she made.

"Looks like that hunk of junk she calls a spaceship is 'down for the count' and requires some repairs," whispered Sparky to Elt.

"What is she doing?" whispered Elt.

"Making a list I think." Klecktonis climbed to the top of her ship. She focused on one particular area. Utilizing her eyes like flashlights, the alien concentrated the light into a specific area that was damaged by the landing. She shut her eyes off and leaped down, landing right in front of Ralph. The startled boy hid behind his super dog.

Klecktonis stretched out her sleek, muscular hand and presented Ralph with her computer. Ralph stepped past Elt to shakily accept her offer. She then turned around and pointed to various sections of her ship. The ship seemed massive; it stood about fifteen feet high and twelve feet wide. Ralph didn't quite understand what this scary creature wanted to relate, for he was still overwhelmed by the sight of her. Trianthians weren't frightening; but she was. Klecktonis, with those powerful lenses, shot a beam of green light across the ship.

Ralph glanced down at the screen and studied its contents. The pictures included some type of shield or sheathing, various forms of plant life, and quite frankly, some objects that the boy had never seen in his life. The alien's presentation to Ralph began to sink in, and now the boy realized why Elt woke him. This strange, terrifying being needed his help. Elt licked the boy's hand. Ralph broke away from the screen and smiled at his dog. Elt required his help, too.

Dawn approached, for the sky began to spew a mixture of violet, orange, and pink, preparing the sun for its morning rise. The crickets and katydids quieted, and the only sound that could be heard was that of Chin relaying bark messages to whoever would hear him. Only Elt and Sparky knew what they meant.

"He wants to know what's going on," whispered Elt.

"We can't honor his wishes at this time dude," related Sparky. Elt nodded in agreement.

Ralph realized what he had to do, but he didn't know where to start. Somehow, he had to locate materials needed to repair the ship. That was his number one priority. The boy didn't know who this scary creature was, but she was on Elt's and Sparky's side; much better than being an adversary. Whether Elt had encountered Klecktonis before Ralph didn't know. He had a challenging mission; find the materials. Hopefully this extra-terrestrial could repair her craft, so the group of heroes could initiate their voyage to Trianthius or wherever they were heading.

"Come on boy," instructed Ralph. "Let's get home before Dad wakes up." Ralph handed the screen back to Klecktonis. He nodded hopefully, to assure her that he was "on the job."

As he walked away, Ralph noticed something at the top of the spaceship, peeking its head in and out. The morning light allowed the boy to recognize who it was. "Oleo," Ralph mouthed to himself as they walked away. "How did he…?"

Ralph had never seen the replicate in his true form for more than a milli-second, but for some reason, knew that the strange being was the Sorgian.

Elt and Jasmine followed Ralph. Sparky remained, for he didn't want to be noticed by anyone within view of Elt's yard. He would have to take chances later that day. Klecktonis stared at the boy and pets; her stoic stature made the others even more confused about what the being was thinking.

Nightfall had transformed into morning, with the dew and fog shimmering on the branches and leaves of the trees. Klecktonis began searching, presumably for the plant life that had something to do with the repair of her ship. She stopped to gaze at Sparky, chirping out a few choice words for him that of course, he didn't understand. Sparky shrugged and returned her glance. "Looks like we have no choice. My human has never let me down." Sparky turned around. Ralph, Elt, and Jasmine were gone.

When the three returned to his backyard, Elt leaped the fence to meet up with Bernadette, who had been patiently waiting all night. She was fatigued, a little hungry, and she still wasn't quite herself. The two canines traded sniffs and kisses. Elt gazed up at his human.

"Go ahead boy, but get back fast," stated Ralph. "We have a lot to do." Ralph headed to the back porch while Elt and Bernadette strolled away together. Jasmine jumped onto the porch and rubbed herself along the boy's pajamas. Ralph sat down to pet the tabby. She began to purr.

How was Ralph going to assist Elt, Sparky, and Klecktonis on the mission? He had managed to venture into the future and rescue his friends. This challenge, just a hundred yards away or so from his backyard, would be a challenge, too. He would have to develop a plan. Trianthius's future depended on it.

CHAPTER 9

THE SPACESHIP FLUTTERED PAST THE Valleydale subdivision. The disruption, barely audible to the human ear, was easily detected by the French Poodle Trixie, who was nestled comfortably at the end of Caroline's bed. Trixie began to bark incessantly.

"Trixie," muttered a half-groggy Caroline. "Be quiet." She tossed and turned, hoping her pooch would stop, but Trixie wouldn't. Protecting her home was usually not high on her list of priorities, but for some reason that night, Trixie was all upset. She had never heard that noise before in her new home, and instincts just took over.

Caroline's brother, Bryan, heard the ruckus and rushed over to calm Trixie. Seymour, the cat with the British accent, slunk in from the living room area. The Londoner, who usually slept in one of the kid's beds, had been sleeping in a secluded spot on a window sill in the front of the house. He also heard the noise, but it didn't alert him. Cats were just more laid back in those types of situations. Now throw a bird, mouse, or fish into the room, and then Seymour, as reserved as he was, would jump into alert mode and pounce on whatever he could. Felines, like dogs, paid attention to familiar noises, such as the front door opening, or the arrival of Mr. Greenlee's vehicle. And there was the ever-pleasant sound of the can opener, which quite frequently meant a delicious meal.

Trixie staggered over to the entrance of Caroline's bedroom, her tail wagging vigorously. She repeated her previous series of barks and yelps. Caroline leaped out of bed. Bryan followed his sister. Professor Greenlee leaned his head inside Caroline's room. "What's all the ruckus about?" He began to yawn.

"Don't know Dad," answered Caroline. "She just keeps barking at something."

The professor bent down to try to assuage Trixie. She stopped barking momentarily, licked Stanley's fingers, and then began to whimper, still visibly upset about something in or around the house. Professor Greenlee rose and headed down the hall en route to the front door. The kids and pets were in close pursuit. He opened the door and stuck his head out to investigate. Stanley stared at the night sky: nothing but darkness. He heard Chin's far-off barking from two houses down. Trixie heard Chin's message and began to cry and yelp all over again.

Stanley stepped out and treaded down the front steps. He detected a slight burning smell, but found no evidence of its source. Trixie was intense, nervous about something in the surrounding area. The professor motioned for Bryan to release her. Trixie raced down the steps and began to sniff the air. She paced back and forth in front of the front gate. "Anything Dad?" asked Bryan.

The professor shook his head no. "Whatever it was, it's gone. Don't know what spooked her." Trixie sniffed the area a few more seconds, and then followed Greenlee back inside the house. "Let's see if we can get a few more winks in tonight children."

The kids and pets followed Stanley down the hall, and then separated into their respective rooms. "I wonder what Trixie heard," stated Caroline. "It's not like her to start a ruckus in the middle of the night."

Bryan shook his head in both agreement and bewilderment. He yawned, and then proceeded to his bedroom. Seymour joined him. Trixie had finally calmed. She jumped back onto Caroline's bed, exhausted from the whole ordeal. She never uttered even a whimper the rest of the evening.

Across the way, Juan the Chihuahua was asleep on Mrs. Perez's bed that evening. His ears perked upwards when the noise passed by above his house, but relaxed when it faded away. Sarge was dreaming of endless fire hydrants that evening before the abrupt noise awakened him. He grumbled for a few moments and paced back and forth between his doggie bed downstairs and the back door. After a moment or two, he lost interest in the disturbance since it was no longer near him. He drifted back to sleep.

Prince the Doberman had contemplated a late night stroll over to the Greenlee's house that evening, hoping to encounter Trixie while the poodle was out on her late night business trip. That plan was thwarted after Mr. Dawkins secured the back door tightly before retiring to bed. The highly decorated canine rested on his living room couch. Even though the sound never actually passed over him, Prince's keen hearing detected something. He performed a series of routine patrols inside the house, but never elected to wake his human. He too, soon fell fast asleep.

Not one human in the Valleydale subdivision heard the disturbance.

CHAPTER 10

RALPH THREW ON A PAIR of shorts, a shirt, and some socks. There was no sense in returning to bed, for sunrise was imminent. Ralph quietly trotted down the hall, skipped into his dad's office, and grabbed a pencil along with a few sheets of notebook paper. He flopped down at the dining room table and began to write. Elt remained by his human the whole time. "Okay," thought Ralph, "what were the things I was supposed to get?"

All the movement from the boy and his dog awakened Mr. Eltison. Elt heard the rustling of the bed covers coming from Mr. Eltison's room. He darted through the doggie door and returned with the newspaper in mere seconds. Mr. Eltison entered the living room yawning, and the noticed his son already awake and dressed. "What's going on this morning?"

Elt wandered over to Mr. Eltison, sat, offered his right paw, and then licked Mr. Eltison's hand when he accepted the canine's offer. "Oh, I'm thinking of building something," replied Ralph. "So I'm writing down all the materials I'm gonna need."

"Building something?" Mr. Eltison was puzzled by Ralph's sudden interest in a construction project, especially before school started. Ralph nodded affirmatively. The boy knew he had to concoct a story, for he didn't want to create any suspicions, especially with an alien spaceship about a football field away from his backyard. "Well, do you know what you're constructing?" quizzed Mr. Eltison. "Is this project for school?"

Ralph shook his head no. "It's not for school, and I haven't decided what I want to create." He paused. "If I find some old pieces of like… metal or wood in the shed, can I use them?"

Ralph's dad wasn't suspicious, just inquisitive. "Well, you need to check with me when you find something. I may have a need for that piece later." Most dads usually kept spare pieces of building materials, just in case.

Elt wasn't quite sure what the conversation was all about, but he knew that Ralph was trying his hardest. He was depending on the boy, and he knew the best chance of completing the mission depended mainly on his young human.

After breakfast, Ralph and Elt poked through the garage and the old shed, searching for the perfect piece of something or other that would help repair the monstrous spaceship. After about ten minutes of close scrutinizing, all the boy could muster was a tiny piece of sheet metal, a couple of boards, and an old coffee can filled with screws. He knew that Elt would have to deliver "the goods," for Ralph had to leave for school.

Ralph and Elt returned inside. The boy dumped some dry dog food into Elt's bowl. Next, he reached into the drawer and retracted a sandwich baggie. He sprinkled more dry food into the bag, and then sealed it. Then he grabbed another sandwich bag and placed two doggie biscuits inside. He handed both bags to Elt. "Go boy, take this bag of food to Sparky, and these treats to Oleo." He remembered that Oleo wasn't too fond of the dry food, but loved the doggie biscuits. Ralph hoped that Sparky would accept his offering.

Elt stared down at the bowl, and then at the two bags Ralph carried in his hand. He snared the bags carefully with his teeth and trotted off through the doggie door. "I have one awesome dog," whispered Ralph to himself. Ralph watched his pooch hasten the pace, gaze back at the house momentarily, and with baggies in mouth, easily jump over the back fence.

Elt delivered the morning goodies to Sparky and Oleo. The canine and the Sorgian were very grateful. "It's not a cheeseburger," proclaimed Sparky, but I'm hungrier than a goat in a coat factory." The canines switched their attention to Klecktonis, who remained close to the ship, but continued her search for plant life and other resources necessary to the repair of her vessel. Ralph hadn't sent any food for her since he had no idea what she might eat.

"I can't recall what she ate the last time we saw her," mentioned Elt.

"No worries," claimed Sparky. "It wasn't human or dog. Besides, she has a collection of weird stuff in that tin can of hers." Sparky pointed to the ship.

"I better get back to my human," said Elt. "I'll return with some supplies."

"See ya later alligator. Hopefully we'll get out of here soon so we can find out what kind of trouble the boss is in."

"Don't you know what's going on?" inquired Elt.

"Remember those dudes with the funny shaped heads, even crazier than that one?" asked Sparky as he pointed in the direction of Klecktonis.

"Oh yeah, the Quadra somethings."

"They have something to do with it," asserted Sparky. "And we need to show up and kick some 'Quadra something' butt."

Elt nodded affirmatively, and then scurried back to his home. Upon his return, Ralph had gathered his book bag and lunch, and headed for the back door. He knelt down to pet his canine. "You know what to do boy?" questioned Ralph. Elt wagged his tail, for he understood his role in this part of the mission. Elt wasn't quite up to par with his human's school schedule, for it was only the second day back. Once he saw Ralph gather his backpack and lunch, the canine knew he was on his own to deliver whatever he could to Klecktonis. Elt was going to have to gather more materials, but a trip to the neighborhood, in the middle of the day, was going to be a challenge. "We'll get that spaceship fixed," assured Ralph. "Man, I wish I could go on this mission." Ralph exited the kitchen. He then stuck his head back inside. "Later Dad."

"Have an awesome day," returned Ralph's dad.

Ralph skipped down the porch and trekked over to Jenny's house. His mind was clearly focused on the situation behind his backyard. Hopefully, everything would stay "status quo" until his return home from school. Staying home or playing sick wasn't an option, for Ralph would be confined to his room. He would be more beneficial to the mission by going to school, and then assisting the crew in the afternoon.

Jenny noticed that Ralph wasn't himself as they walked to class. Her friend wasn't the first one to act strange that morning. She awoke to discover her Bernadette outside, staring at the next yard, and whimpering. After repeated attempts to call her inside, Jenny had to run to her Cocker Spaniel and calm her. Before the two kids reached Bryan and Caroline's house, Jenny could sense that her friend was deep in thought. "What ya thinking about?" questioned Jenny.

Ralph wanted to "spill the beans" right then and there, but he knew he couldn't. He had kept Elt's powers a secret from Jenny for quite some time. There were mysteries involving Bernadette, too. He had to remain quiet, for the mission depended on it. "Oh, I was just working on a project at home," replied Ralph. "I can't find all the materials I need to finish the project."

"Maybe we have some stuff you can use at my house," Jenny offered. "Can I help?"

"Oh no, why did I say what I just said?" thought Ralph as he desperately tried to figure a way to wriggle out of this sticky situation. Luckily, the discussion was interrupted by the Greenlee children's arrival. Caroline and Bryan walked behind their friends as they headed to the elementary school.

"Hey, me dad is conducting experiments on a gigantic telescope at the observatory," reported Bryan.

"It's true," confirmed Caroline. "He's going to show us planets, solar systems, and stars."

Jenny shook her head. "Your dad has the coolest job ever. First, you get to travel with him on the time machine. Now, you'll discover new and exciting worlds with this telescope."

"We are lucky," admitted Caroline.

Although Ralph's mind wasn't on the conversation at hand, his dad too, had a pretty cool job. For one, his dad was able to stay at home so he could spend more time with Ralph. Secondly, Ralph was able to venture out sometimes for "field trips" with his dad while Mr. Eltison either ran errands or visited clients. These trips, however, didn't involve a time machine.

But none of these thoughts mattered. An alien, a replicate, and a canine from San Francisco were stranded behind his backyard. He had helped rescue his friends twenty-five years into the future. What was going to happen to Elt and his friends this time? How long would Elt be gone once the ship was repaired? Where were the space heroes headed? Where were the Trianthians? They were always present for the missions, or at least involved in some way.

Ralph attempted to stay focused in class, but he wasn't very successful. There were no daydreams, but Ralph was distracted, in deep thought. Mr. Campbell could have discussed the most interesting topic that day but it wouldn't have mattered. Ralph couldn't wait for the school day to end. Soon he would exit through the front doors, walk home with his friends, and tend to the mission at hand.

CHAPTER 11

"WHAT IS SHE DOING?" ASKED one super dog to the other.

"I think she's searching for fuel," returned the other.

Klecktonis roamed about, not far from her ship. Her greenish-blue hue blended magnificently with the leafy foliage that surrounded her. In one of her hands she held her computer. She examined a scattering of leaves, searching for a match, or something sensibly close. She even tasted a select few of the samples.

Daylight had aided her quest for the desired resources, but it also posed the threat of being discovered by a human or another creature in the woods. The longer the alien remained behind Ralph's yard, the more precarious Klecktonis's situation was.

"I think you should deliver your goodies," proceeded Jasmine.

"Smart thinking," returned Elt. In a flash, he vanished, and then re-appeared with the materials that Ralph had gathered. Although he possessed extraordinary strength, Elt had to make several trips, for he could only fit so much in his clenched jaws. He discarded the scrap pieces in front of the ship.

Klecktonis chewed on some honeysuckle petals, a favorite also of the Trianthians. She glided over to the spot where Elt had discarded the materials. She bent down and rummaged through the pile. The alien examined the one section of scrap metal, bending it in multiple directions. She motioned with her hands that she required more of that kind of sheet metal. Unfortunately, that was the only parcel that Elt had delivered.

"What do we do?" worried Jasmine. "I think she needs more."

Sparky and Elt remained silent for a moment, but then Sparky's eyes widened. "Your team, anyone we can visit?" asked the Golden Retriever.

"I guess," thought Elt with growing excitement. "But we'll have to be careful. Do you want to come with us?"

Sparky nodded his head yes. "Dude, I'm so bored back here. Besides, even though we're on the same team," Sparky glanced one more time at Klecktonis, who now was matching up the piece of metal to a damaged spot on her spaceship, "she still creeps me out."

"We know what you mean," chimed in Jasmine.

The three pets slithered cautiously past Elt's backyard and headed for the front. "Wait, let's go this way," instructed Jasmine, referring to her backyard. "My human isn't home." Jasmine had noticed that her human's transport vehicle was missing. Mrs. Reed was a librarian at the Spring Valley Public Library.

Sparky, Elt, and Jasmine hurriedly hurdled the fence and dashed through Jasmine's yard, stopping at Mrs. Reed's shed. Elt pushed the door open. It was dark, but a splattering of light filtered through, enabling the group to view the objects stored in Mrs. Reed's shed. Sparky fished through a couple of piles while Elt and Jasmine pawed through wood and metal scraps around a workbench.

Suddenly the retriever called out, "I think I found something!"

Elt inspected the larger pieces of aluminum Sparky had found. "All she can say is no. Let's take 'em." Elt and Sparky carried mouthfuls of the metals and placed them just outside the shed door. Elt sniffed in the direction of Chin's yard. He spotted Mrs. Yao's garage, but it was very close to the house and Mrs. Yao was probably home. Venturing into Chin's yard would be too risky. The group swiftly crossed the street. Sarge had just come around the corner of his house when he noticed his friends, but who was that stranger with them? Sarge began to bark. Elt dashed over to the fence. "Shhhh," he scowled. "Are you trying to alert the whole neighborhood?"

Sarge rushed closer. He shook himself, but that retriever was still there, in plain view. "Who in tarnation is that?" he demanded, confused.

Sparky sensed no tension or hostility in Sarge. He strutted ahead of the group. "Just the most righteous retriever in the state of California."

"This is Sparky," interrupted Elt. "He's from......I mean.....he lives far away."

Sparky slid his paw through one of the fence holes. The Boxer didn't quite understand Sparky's motive. "Okay then," remarked the retriever as he withdrew his gesture.

"We're searching for some things your humans may own," interjected Elt.

"Things? What things?" Sarge's nose never stopped sniffing in Sparky's direction. "You can't have my collection of hidden bones or my blankie," stated Sarge with finality.

"Not those things silly," meowed Jasmine softly. "Stuff like, you know, that would help repair an alien space transporter, something like that."

"Alien space transporter?" ruffed Sarge. "You mean that funny looking space guy is back? I do not want to travel in any of those machines again!"

"More like a space gal," commented Sparky.

"Never mind that," interrupted Elt. "Can we go sniffing around the old meeting place?"

Sarge nervously surveyed the area, and then gazed back at the old toolshed, the former site of the neighborhood pet meetings. "I hope my human doesn't find out about this." Sarge pointed to the house. "He's in the house right now, and loves to watch me out here."

"We'll be quick," assured Jasmine. Within seconds, all four pets were inside the shed. Attempting to remain as silent as possible, the three pooches and one feline pawed through a plethora of wood, metal, and fiberglass scraps.

"I think this will do," smiled Elt.

"This one looks righteous," Sparky nodded with pride.

The pets crept out of the toolshed with their mouths full. Trixie had just skipped down the front steps when she caught a glimpse of Elt and Sparky easily jumping over Sarge's fence. Seymour, who was just a step or two behind the poodle, stopped in his tracks. Trixie's initial instinct was to bark at the duo, but she held back. Luckily, Mrs. Greenlee had not noticed the two extra dogs when she opened the door for her pooch and feline to take care of business that morning.

"Who is that gorgeous one?" mused Trixie, referring to the handsome Golden Retriever across the street from her. Trixie and Seymour watched as Sarge paced nervously back and forth in his yard, hoping that Mr. Davis wouldn't open the front door and discover all the pets jumping over his fence and scurrying about. They saw Sparky and Elt zoom to Jasmine's yard, while the tabby didn't even attempt to catch up. No one in the group even noticed their friends across the way.

"Do you feel like you're going slower than usual?" barked Elt through the load of metal in his mouth.

"Maybe," huffed Sparky. The delivery of all the scrap materials was accomplished in about three trips for both super dogs. Klecktonis poked through the piles and closely inspected each piece. She discarded most of them.

"She's a picky one," commented Jasmine.

"I better go check on my older human," cautioned Elt.

"Looks like we're not going anywhere anyway," stated Sparky.

Elt bolted away and returned home. He found Mr. Eltison in his office, speaking on the phone with one of his clients. Sniffing the area, Elt stepped into the office. Then he moved gracefully under Ralph's dad's outstretched hand to receive an ear scratching.

At school, Ralph had a hard time focusing on his studies. Thoughts of Sparky, Oleo and that strange alien filled his mind. Since there was no visit from his dad, or possibly Sheriff Thomas, the group in the woods must still be safe and undiscovered. Ralph was unsure if he provided enough raw materials for the space traveler, and he couldn't wait to find out.

When the dismissal bell did ring, Ralph resisted the urge to jet home. Racing home without walking with his friends might have aroused suspicions; he needed to remain calm, maybe just walk a little speedier than normal.

"Elt and I might not be able to walk today," declared Ralph, awkwardly trying to sound natural. Jenny noticed Ralph was walking faster, but didn't think much of it.

"That's okay," she responded. "I'll have to see how Bernadette is feeling. We may be going to the vet's office today, anyway."

"We may be visiting the veterinarian's office today as well," interjected Caroline. "Trixie was acting really strange last night."

"Yeah, so was Bernie," added Jenny. "It's not like her to whimper and not answer me when I call for her." As Ralph pressed onward, he tried to recall Bernadette's demeanor when he saw her the night before. It was dark, but she had seemed fine.

When the kids reached Jenny's house, Bryan stopped. "Hey, did you hear any strange noises in the night, last night?"

"Yeah, like an airplane or something?" added Caroline.

Ralph's eyes widened. What did they know? Did they know anything at all? "I didn't hear anything," he said, trying to dismiss it.

"I think we heard something," said Caroline. "Maybe it was a UFO. Dad has been searching for one on his telescope, you know?"

"Trixie heard it too," reported Bryan. "She woke us up from our sleep." Ralph started to perspire, and not just because it was warm outside. His friends were onto something. "Stay calm," he thought to himself.

"I must have been really pooped," added Jenny. "I didn't hear a sound, and Bernie didn't wake up either." What Jenny didn't realize was the whereabouts of her Bernadette the night before. If she would have awakened, Jenny would have noticed that her dog was missing.

"Me dad looked, but didn't see anything," added Bryan. "I really wanted it to be a UFO." Bryan grinned.

"That would be something," smiled Ralph nervously. "Well, I better head home and check on Elt. See you all tomorrow!"

"Cheerio!" gleamed Bryan.

"Trixie! Seymour!" exclaimed Caroline as she opened her gate.

"Bye," waved Jenny. She too was worried, not about a weird noise or a UFO, but whether or not her pooch was feeling better.

Ralph ran the rest of the way home. He discovered Elt resting on the back porch, staring at the woods. He dropped his backpack, checked for his dad, and then trekked over to the back fence. Elt bounded along and Ralph followed him into the woods. Klecktonis and Sparky were busy collecting plant life. Ralph couldn't determine whether the ship had been repaired in any certain areas, for the ship was scarred in several places, most likely due to many voyages into not-so-desirable atmospheres. He did notice that the ship was easier to spot now that daylight was present.

The alien sighted Ralph and immediately clamored over to her ship to point out the areas that still required attention. Ralph gazed down at the ground. There were various pieces of metal and wood strewn about the landing area. Sparky dropped shrubbery off near the ship and joined Elt and Ralph.

The boy edged closer and touched the ship. Although Coladeus had visited him twice in the Trianthian space pod, Ralph never had the chance to discover what an alien ship felt like. The outer surface of Klecktonis's ship was cool despite a very hot summer afternoon. Ralph couldn't determine what the outer shell of the ship felt like; was it metal, vinyl, or plastic? Could it have been some type of alloy? Perhaps that was why the alien couldn't utilize the supplies that were on the ground.

Ralph wracked his brain. How could they help? One human, two dogs, one feline, and a very intimidating alien needed to conquer the challenge. Ralph brainstormed. And then he had an idea. "Come on boy," he urged. Elt followed his human quickly back to the house.

CHAPTER 12

"You really need to go now?" asked Mr. Eltison. The boy and his dad climbed into the truck. "Did you make a decision on what you're building?

"I want to construct something better than a boat or an airplane," explained Ralph. "Maybe a submarine or... a spaceship."

Mr. Eltison's work day was basically over. He didn't mind taking his son to the hardware store, but he was a little perplexed about Ralph's sudden interest in this construction project, especially during the school year. "And you have enough money to purchase what you need?" He turned the key in the ignition.

Ralph reached into his pockets and withdrew a fistful of balled-up dollar bills along with a collection of coins. "I think I have enough."

Before Ralph had requested the visit to Feldman's Hardware, Ralph and Elt had headed straight for the money jar in Ralph's room. There seemed to be enough cash to cover the expense, but who knew? Ralph had no clue what construction materials would cost.

"And you're sure you don't require my assistance on the construction?" inquired Mr. Eltison a bit skeptically. Ralph recognized his dad's hesitance. The boy wasn't the type of kid that built things. Lego castles and Lincoln Log homes, sure, but Ralph didn't tinker too much with projects "from scratch." "Well ok then, off to Feldman's," proclaimed Mr. Eltison as he backed the pickup out of the driveway.

Feldman's Hardware offered an array of tools, hardware, lawn care products, and garden accessories, along with a limited supply of lumber and building materials. If anyone in Spring Valley carried the materials necessary to mend an alien spacecraft, it would be Feldman's. A right on Main Street, and then a left just past the Palace Theatre, brought them to ample parking in the rear of the hardware store. The Eltisons whisked past Henry Buttersample, who was out in front of his candy emporium, handing out samples of the peanut butter fudge that Mrs. Buttersample had just baked. Henry noticed Ralph and Elt in the passenger seat of the truck and waved. He watched the truck pull into the alley and then disappear. The memories of the time machine, the trip into the future, and the boy with his dog were fresh in his memory, but weren't connectable. Henry turned around and offered a piece of fudge to the next passerby.

Mr. Feldman was re-organizing a few of his late summer sales displays when Ralph, his dad, and Elt pushed open the jingle belled door into the hardware store. Now pets weren't typically allowed at the store, but because Elt was one of the Valleydale Pet Heroes, the pooch, along with any other of the Valleydale pets and their owners, were welcomed with open arms.

"Ah, it's Mr. Ralph and his amazing dog," heralded Mr. Feldman. "How can I help you this fine afternoon?"

Ralph was caught off guard by the generous greeting. Mr. Eltison smiled and stepped forward. "Ralph is working on a project, but I'm not sure what type of building materials he's looking for."

Ralph snapped out of his shyness. "Do you have sheets of metal or really tough plastic?"

"Certainly my good man," answered Mr. Feldman, cheerily. The store owner escorted the Eltisons two aisles over. Elt accompanied his humans to the sheet metal display. Ralph was amazed at how many different shapes and sizes of metal were showcased at Feldman's. There were square ones, rectangular, corrugated, and some with lattices.

Ralph had no clue. There were so many styles. Which one should he pick? He only remembered roughly what size it was supposed to be. He didn't want to disappoint the alien and Sparky. The repair of the spaceship and continuation of the mission rested on the ten year-old's shoulders. He depended on his super dog for the solution.

"Which one boy?" he whispered. The canine sniffed an assortment of styles, and then honed in on one particular piece of steel. "This one?" asked Ralph. Elt wagged his tail excitedly.

"Is Elt choosing your piece for you?" laughed Mr. Feldman. The store owner began to scratch his head.

"Looks like he is," shrugged Mr. Eltison.

"That is one intelligent dog," grinned Mr. Feldman. Ralph smiled at his dad. He checked the price of the metal.

"Do you have enough money to pay for that piece?" asked Ralph's dad.

Ralph rummaged through his pockets and withdrew the wad of one dollar bills and some coins. He nodded yes. "I might need a couple of bucks."

Mr. Feldman smiled. "I think we can accommodate you. Your intelligent, wonderful dog helped save our town. I think I can knock two dollars off the price of that sheet metal."

"Thanks Mr. Feldman," said a very grateful Ralph. He moved toward the register and handed over his money. The hardware store owner rang up the sale and then leaned over to pat Elt.

"Please let me know how your project turns out, son. Bring pictures." He grinned and waved as the Eltisons jingled out of the store.

Within minutes, they arrived at home. "I'll start dinner," informed Mr. Eltison. "Do you have any homework, or are you going to work on your project?" Ralph did have homework, but Trianthius's very existence was at stake. He had to deliver the sheet metal to the mission team.

"I'm going to work on the project," he said more confidently than he felt. "Can I use the shed?"

"Just be careful, and clean up after yourself when you're finished."

"Thanks Dad. Come on boy." Ralph clutched the sheet metal and headed out the back door. Elt trailed behind his human by a couple of canine steps. The two had to remain careful, for Ralph's dad was cooking in the kitchen. Just one glance out the window and catching Ralph and Elt crossing into the woods would sabotage the entire mission.

Ralph unlocked the shed door and entered. The boy peered back toward the house. He didn't see his dad. "Don't get caught," he thought to himself. Cautiously, he handed the metal to his dog. Elt zoomed away, jumped over the fence and darted off into the woods. Ralph glanced back one more time, then made his move. He scaled the fence, and disappeared.

As Ralph reached the spaceship site, he suddenly slowed and his mouth fell open. Klecktonis was already working on the affected area of her ship with the new piece of metal. But it was *how* she was completing the repair that amazed Ralph, Jasmine and even Elt and Sparky. The alien held the piece of metal up against the vessel. Then her laser eyes began to glow brighter and brighter. The blinding beams of light struck the metal and welded it instantly.

Ralph couldn't believe what he had just witnessed. Sparky and Elt had viewed a similar scene on Titan, but it was still pretty amazing to watch again.

Within minutes, Olco stood beside Elt, and with Klecktonis's assistance, was transformed again into the new Elt. Ralph sighed and bent down to hug his dog. He realized that he wouldn't be able to attend the mission, that his part once again was to carry on like normal with Elt's replicate. Sparky moved over to Ralph and gave his hand an encouraging lick. The boy returned the favor by hugging the Golden Retriever.

Klecktonis prepared her spaceship. She deposited foliage into her fuel tank. Hopefully, it would be enough to sustain a trip into deep space.

"Dinner time, Ralph," the boy heard his father in the distance. Ralph collected a few scraps of metal that were lying around. Before he walked away, Ralph turned around in time to watch both his dog and Sparky fly to the top of the ship.

"Be careful boy," Ralph whispered to himself. "You too Sparky. I hope to see you again." When he reached the back fence, Ralph helped the new Elt over the fence, threw the scrap pieces into his yard, and climbed over. He gathered the scraps neatly and piled them in an area underneath Mr. Eltison's workbench. He wasn't too worried about what he was going to construct; he and the new Elt would figure out something the next day. The spaceship's departure had been the ultimate goal.

While he ate dinner, Ralph watched Oleo, who was already familiar with the routine. Ralph wondered what was happening in the woods. How he desired to just run back there to assist, but he couldn't compromise the mission.

It was close to midnight when a loud sustained noise awakened Mr. Eltison. For a short time, that strange, low hum was part of his dream. But when he fully awoke, Ralph's dad realized that it was originating from outside. By the time he arrived at the back porch, however, the noise was gone. Only faint barks from Chin and Sarge could be heard. Jasmine rushed up to Mr. Eltison and brushed against his leg. He bent down and rubbed her scruff.

"Dad, what's going on?" yawned Ralph. The boy had attempted to stay up late, but finally succumbed to his fatigue. The new Elt remained by Ralph's side.

"I thought I heard a noise outside," answered Ralph's dad. "I'm surprised Elt didn't pick up on it. You guys must have been exhausted."

"I didn't hear anything," returned Ralph as he scratched his head. But inside he was gleeful, for he knew that the spaceship had departed. That had to have been the noise his dad heard. Elt, Sparky, and Klecktonis were now on their way to Trianthius.

Earlier that evening, Klecktonis had secured the lid to the spaceship. "Stay down below buddy," insisted Sparky. There were just two seats up top. "We'll trade up later so you can see the sights. Believe me, if it's anything like the first trip, you don't really want to see what's going on."

The alien pushed a sequence of buttons. Small doors opened above Sparky's head and to the right side of Elt; out popped oxygen masks. Elt nudged his nose under the flaps of his mask and adjusted the straps with his paws. Mission accomplished. Well, not really. "Impressive," commented Sparky. He took the cue from Elt to slip on his own oxygen mask.

It was night, just before midnight in fact. Klecktonis and her crew were ready to blast off, out into deep space. Unbeknownst to the travelers, however, before Klecktonis sealed the door, a stowaway had entered, fluttering its way inside and attaching itself to an interior wall of the spaceship. The survival of that stowaway on board was key to the survival of the Trianthian existence.

CHAPTER 13

THE SCIENTIST WILLED HIMSELF UPWARDS off the floor of his laboratory. He was weak, and his sight was impaired significantly. He mustered enough strength to secure a seat by his control panel, which contained a three-dimensional holographic screen which stored all of his formulas, theories, and notes.

Coughing and wheezing, he attempted to engage the picture, but the deficiency of power caused the picture to malfunction. Determined to continue on, the scientist waddled over to a desk-type structure made of tree-roots. Inside his desk were several naturally-made cubby areas. Nestled in those cubbies were scores of old scrolls. He reached into the middle of the collection and nabbed two four-fingered handfuls. He set them down on the desk and began to scan them one by one.

"Mogulus, is that you?" asked another being who had just walked into the scientist's laboratory. The Trianthian mastermind, who not too long ago had calculated a way for Coladeus and his spaceship to travel through time without the use of a time machine, glanced back only for a second. Determined, Mogulus forged on.

Kraylen, a Trianthian elder and fellow council member, struggled to walk a few paces closer to the researcher and inventor. "What are you researching?" he asked in his alien dialect.

Mogulus hauled another stack of scrolls to his desk, sifting through each one of them hastily. "Since the virtual command center is down, due to lack of crystal energy, something in these scrolls may hold the key to how the Quadrasones penetrated our force field and are draining our resources."

Mogulus was correct. The Quadrasones had perfected some type of device that not only pierced through the seemingly impenetrable Trianthian force-field, but was also draining the planet and its inhabitants of its natural resource. If Mogulus couldn't find an answer to this problem, the power generated by the Trianthian crystals would diminish and leave the planet and the Trianthians to perish. The scientist figured he had some morsel of information in those papers; a clue that might just save their existence.

The Trianthian force-field was a defense mechanism, a shield used to secure and protect the planet from outside dangers. Designed by Trianthian engineers before the time of Mogulus and Coladeus, the defense system was supported by eight different power plants throughout the planet, so there wouldn't be any weak points in any one area of the system. Invisible rays, with similar strength as the litoses rays, all converged on each other from the eight stations to create one omnipresent blanket of protection.

What did the force-field prevent? Mainly outside intruders. Trianthius was a peaceful civilization, yet the Trianthians had to protect themselves. With crews to fill only three spaceships and no substantial military force, the Trianthians could easily fall prey to an aggressive species.

"Have we received any transmissions from Coladeus?" asked Mogulus as he continued to rummage through the almost endless rows of materials at his disposal.

"We believe that he is aware of the current situation," returned Kraylen. "He is our only hope, unless you can somehow devise a plan to reverse our current situation."

Mogulus's eyes brightened for a second or two. A sudden burst of energy overcame him as the inventor rolled out a scroll onto his desk. "We may have something here."

*   *   *

It was a restless evening of sleep for the ten year-old. Only a few hours had transpired since his super dog had embarked on possibly his most crucial mission. It was difficult for Ralph to fall asleep. Soon he would have to dig himself out of bed, make sure his replicate retrieved the newspaper, feed Oleo and himself breakfast, and start a new, challenging day in Mr. Campbell's class.

Oleo had memorized the routine; it hadn't been that long since he once occupied Ralph's bed. Ralph recalled Oleo's habits too. When Ralph awakened, the newspaper was already sitting on Mr. Eltison's chair. The boy reached for the dry dog food by habit, but then changed directions to where the doggie treats were located. The lad nabbed a couple of the treats, crumbled them into tinier pieces, and spread them into Elt's bowl. The replicate kindly obliged by scarfing up the morsels in mere seconds.

Ralph checked the water level in Elt's bowl. Ralph attempted to recall one characteristic of the Sorgian. Did he drink water? Was it required to sustain life? "Oh well. Let's just make sure it stays full," thought Ralph to himself.

Although it still was difficult allowing Elt to depart on another mission, the feeling in his stomach wasn't as unsettling this time. He trusted Sparky and Elt. He wasn't quite sure about the alien with the laser-beam eyes. Klecktonis was an ally, but he wasn't quite sure of the alien's intentions and to what lengths she would go to protect Elt and Sparky.

Mr. Eltison read the paper while he ate his breakfast. He suspected nothing, except he was still curious about what his son was constructing in the shed. He wanted to take a peek, but respected his son's privacy.

"When can I view your masterpiece?" he smiled.

The boy had to fib; it was critical to the mission. He hated lying to his dad though. He hesitated momentarily, and then collected his thoughts. "I need to finish up," spouted Ralph. "When it's complete, you'll be the first one to see it."

Ralph's dad smiled. "Sounds exciting, I'm honored to be the first to see your work of art."

"Great, what am I going to create?" thought Ralph to himself as he poured the cereal into his bowl. Once he finished breakfast, Ralph hugged his dog and gathered his books. Soon he was out the door, on his way to Jenny's house. There were no worries, for Ralph was sure that Oleo knew how to "lay low" and just be a dog while the boy attended school.

"I want to show you something," said Jenny as she ushered her friend over to the backyard. Bernadette was lying in the grass, facing the Greenlee's backyard. Jasmine the tabby was perched on the fence beside the Cocker Spaniel.

"Bernie, come here girl," requested Jenny.

Just a few minutes earlier, Bernadette had remained outside while Jenny ate breakfast and dressed for school. The spaniel nibbled on a select patch of grass while Jasmine leaped onto the fence. "The giant space transporter flew away last night," reported Jasmine.

"Does that mean…?" worried Bernadette.

"Elt is gone," assured Jasmine. "And his creepy copy dog is back."

"Do you know how long they'll be gone?" inquired Bernadette. "I really had to tell him something."

Jasmine nodded no. "You didn't see how monstrous that transporter was, and who was controlling it. Elt and Sparky flew to the top, which I must say was pretty impressive. That was the last time I saw them."

Bernadette, saddened by Elt's departure, hung her head low and began to grapple with a few more blades of grass.

"Are you feeling okay?" questioned Jasmine.

"That's why I wanted to see Elt before he left," replied Bernadette.

With Ralph beside her, Jenny called for Bernadette.

"Gotta go," jetted Bernadette. She ran as swiftly as she could. When Bernadette reached Jenny, the girl hugged her spaniel. Ralph examined Bernadette while rubbing her neck. Bernadette returned the gesture with a few doggie kisses on his hand.

"What's the matter with her?" asked Ralph. "She seems fine to me."

"I don't know," answered Jenny. "She's not eating as much. She doesn't seem like herself….lethargic. Mom says that if she still feels the same way by the time we get home, we're gonna take her to the vet's office." The kids began to rub Bernadette's belly. Nothing physical appeared unusual about the Cocker Spaniel. Ralph massaged her belly vigorously, for that's what he did with his dog.

"Be gentle," directed Jenny. Ralph rubbed Bernadette more gently. Being close to Jenny's dog helped Ralph forget about his current situation. He loved to pet Elt's belly. How he wanted to share Elt's secrets with his friend, even Bernadette's adventures too. "We better get going," gestured Jenny. "I'm sure Caroline and Bryan are waiting for us." Jenny grabbed the rest of her materials. "Bye Mom!" she shouted. The kids headed out the back door.

"Hey, once Bernadette feels better, we can go on walks again," offered Jenny.

"Sure," replied Ralph a bit reluctantly. He truly treasured the time he spent with Jenny, Elt, and the Cocker Spaniel walking almost every day. But now Ralph would have to walk Oleo, which presented its own challenges of keeping the replicate's identity a secret. If Bernadette was unable to walk for a couple of days, then that situation might help Ralph buy some time until his dog returned.

"I was thinking," continued Jenny, "that when she does feel better, we should walk down Spring Drive instead. You know, mix things up a little and visit some new neighbors."

Jenny and Ralph scurried over to the Greenlee's house. Caroline and Bryan hugged Seymour and Trixie as the two kids walked out their front door. "We saw you in your backyard with Bernadette," noted Bryan. "Is she okay?"

Jenny updated the Greenlee kids on the latest news relating to her dog. Ralph's mind was ablaze with many thoughts. Safety for Elt, Oleo, Bernadette, Coladeus, and Sparky was the first of his concerns. The friends conversed while they trekked their way to school. Ralph wished for his dog's safe return that afternoon, but he knew it was way too soon.

CHAPTER 14

TRIANTHIUS I DECREASED ITS SPEED as it approached its destination. The shock of the crew, including their captain's, had been substantiated. The Trianthians on board now knew what had occurred exactly, but still couldn't ascertain why.

"We're approaching Trianthius sir," Matheun reported as he watched the events before him in disbelief.

"Let's proceed with caution," authorized Coladeus in his Trianthian dialect. "With favor, can you gather any and all information regarding that warship and the force field it's generating?"

"I don't understand sir," lamented Mathuen. "The history surrounding the Quadrasonian race reveals that when they attempt to engage in a plan of destruction, they usually remain 'in the shadows,' not openly attacking the planet and its citizens."

Coladeus paused momentarily. "Evidently, total annihilation is their leader's plan."

"Zemak?" inquired Matheun.

"I understand that he has been their leader for quite some time now," stated Coladeus. "He has evidently developed a weapon so formidable, that it has the capability to penetrate our defense system and drain our planet, our home, of every ounce of its resources."

Matheun studied his screen. "Of what we can decipher, the Quadrasone's warship is composed of a rare alloy of various metals. Their ship is cavernous, with multiple levels; mostly operational, mechanical, and scientific."

"No living quarters?" asked Coladeus.

"Negative," responded the first officer.

"The Quadrasones don't require a space to rest?" questioned Coladeus.

"It is quite possible that they are able to 'shut down' in their place of work," chimed Matheun.

Coladeus pushed a button on his console. A holographic image appeared in front of him. He thought for a moment. He was weak. His thought processes were deteriorating. The Quadrasonian warship and Trianthius II were in plain view; that meant that they were too.

"The ray that their ship is firing," started Coladeus, "it's powerful enough to render our planet and Trianthius II helpless."

"We now know why we never received an adequate transmission from Trianthius II," analyzed Matheun.

"Are there any life readings on board Trianthius II?" asked the captain.

Matheun scanned the situation on board Trianthius II. "Life readings are very low sir," reported the first officer. "However, no casualties at this time."

"That's excellent news," exhaled Coladeus. "Have we been able to establish communications with either the ship or Trianthius?"

"We have received no transmissions at this time," returned Matheun.

"My original plan was to wait for reinforcements," stated the captain in the Trianthian dialect. "But I'm not sure if that's going to happen. Do we have enough power to fire a series of litoses rays upon their vessel, even for a very short period of time?"

Mathuen turned around to face his captain. "Sir, if we fire upon the Quadrasones, it will certainly wipe out any energy that we have remaining. We will have to draw closer."

The captain was sure that Trianthius I's presence had been detected, yet there was no sign of an attack by the Quadrasones. Trianthius I slowly drew closer to the warship. Matheun delivered the coordinates for the attack. He then turned around to face his captain. The rest of the Trianthian crew, barely moving at all, watched their leader make possibly one of his last decisions.

"What choice do we have at this point?" Coladeus reasoned. He paused. "Are we in optimum firing distance?" Mathuen nodded. "Commence firing," he directed quietly. But before Trianthius I could initiate the offensive, Trianthius I was thrust against its will, as if it was being pulled by a magnetic force. The huge beam of light that had encompassed the planet and one of its spaceships now included Trianthius I.

"We're unable to fire!" shouted Matheun.

Trianthius I shook and shimmied its way to the Quadrasonian ship. As it passed by its sister vessel, Coladeus and his crew could only imagine the mutual feelings coming from Trianthius II of desperation and helplessness.

"What action shall we pursue?" urged the first officer. Although there was protocol for such an event, Mathuen had never actually experienced a situation like the one the crew was in now.

Coladeus was calm. "I will have to board their ship and surrender."

Almost instantly, Zemak's holographic image appeared before Coladeus and his crew. No words were spoken. Coladeus rose, exited the bridge, and headed for the transport modules.

CHAPTER 15

THE TWELVE YEAR-OLD WATCHED HER pet run. He fetched a Frisbee and returned it to her. There was nothing unusual about his appearance. But something just wasn't right. This wasn't the first time she felt that way. The difference, and it was key, was that at times the replicate was squeamish when it came to entering the water. After several minutes of begging and prodding, the new Sparky would finally jump into the water. The surfboard, however, was a different story. Amy thought it strange that at times, Sparky refused to climb on board the thing that she thought he truly loved.

"Rat," as the Sorgian was dubbed by Sparky, had difficulties professing his love for the water and especially surfboarding. There was a distinct difference between his and Sparky's abilities on the board, and the distinction had nothing to do with super powers. Rat dreaded the encounters and his hesitation of both entering the water and riding the waves would confuse and frustrate Amy.

After the game of fetch, Amy Pendergrass decided to walk over to her dad's surf shop. "Coconut Waves," her dad's pride and joy, was only about a mile from her home.

"You notice anything different about Sparky lately Dad?" asked Amy.

Kyle Pendergrass continued to wax the surfboard that was in front of him, but Amy's question made him slow a bit. "Nothing unusual. Why? What's going on with your 'radical retriever?'"

Perplexed, Amy shook her head. "I don't know, it's very strange the way he acts sometimes. He just doesn't seem like himself."

Kyle examined the board's flawless shine. "Hmm. You know, we don't feel like ourselves all the time, either."

Amy thought for a few seconds. "But aren't dogs supposed to be happy all the time?"

There was truth to her statement and her father realized it. No matter what mood a human was in, a canine was generally there to perk up his or her spirits. There was always a wagging tail or an array of doggie kisses to share. "I'll have to check and see if it's time for a vet appointment," agreed Amy's dad. "Maybe he needs some dog vitamins or something."

"Sparky has a healthy appetite," mentioned Amy. Unlike his fellow Sorgian, Oleo, who only munched on doggie biscuits, Rat enjoyed a wider variety of canine cuisine. The replicate would even wolf-down an occasional cheeseburger or two thrown his way.

The girl bent down and hugged her retriever. She rubbed his hair. In response, the dog first licked her hands, and then her forehead. She examined her canine's ears. All clear. Amy made sure that Sparky's collar wasn't too tight, but not too loose either. She didn't check the inside of his collar. Sparky always kept the stone hidden. Since she left his collar on when they swam, Amy never bothered to take off the collar when it was Sparky's bath time. It would soon be time for a new collar, although the neckpiece on the replicate looked newer. "I guess it doesn't need changing," thought Amy.

"Hey, you wanna help me do some stuff around here?" asked Mr. Pendergrass.

"Sure," Amy answered resolutely.

"You can move some of that stuff in those boxes onto the shelf over there and maybe sweep some."

Amy nodded and headed over to the front area of the store. Business was a little slow that day, but from time to time, a customer would pop in, and Kyle Pendergrass would walk away from his tasks and assist the patrons. Amy swept the floor and hung around for about an hour before gathering her things to head home. Her dad handed her a couple of bucks for a snack on the way home.

"See you at dinner Dad," Amy shouted as she stepped out the back door with the new Sparky.

"See ya, Kiddo," responded Kyle.

Amy and Sparky ambled home. She worried about the strange way her dog acted at times, but had no idea that the Sorgian replicate was saving her a deeper worry. Her very own dog was struggling to save the Trianthian race, along with his very own life.

CHAPTER 16

"GET HERE AS FAST AS you can," begged Jenny. That was the phone message Ralph received. What was going on? He had just seen Jenny a couple of hours ago when he walked home with her, Bryan, and Caroline. "Make sure you bring Elt too," she continued. What was all the excitement about?

Ralph's curiosity suddenly consumed him. His plan for the rest of the day had been to complete his homework and finish his home project that lay scattered about in his shed. What was so important that he and Elt had to come visit her? Ralph was perplexed.

The boy explained Jenny's call to his father. Typically, it was about the same time of the day that the kids walked their pets anyway.

"Can I go over and see what's going on?" asked Ralph.

"Is your homework finished?" asked Mr. Eltison. "What about your chores?"

Ralph's completed homework was already nestled inside his homework folder in his book bag. There were no more chores for him until after supper when the dishes called his name. Before the call, he had been formulating some blueprint of what he was going to create in the shed.

After Mr. Eltison's approval, Oleo accompanied Ralph on the trip to Jenny's place. When he and his dog arrived, Bryan and Caroline were already seated, with Trixie and Seymour lying in the grass near the side porch. "So, what's going on?" queried Ralph. The boy stood while the new Elt found a spot a few yards away from the other pets. Trixie's ears perked when she noticed the boy and his dog approach. As he passed by her, Oleo allowed the poodle to sniff him. She couldn't put her paw on it, but something wasn't quite right with Elt. She kept her mouth shut and watched.

"We haven't a clue," chimed Caroline.

"We thought you might know," suggested Bryan.

Ralph shrugged his shoulders.

"Jenny said she would be out in a jiffy," explained Caroline. "But that was a while ago, so I'm not sure how long a jiffy is."

Trixie was on edge, and wanted to growl. But she had an image to protect. She had definitely acted out of character the night the strange noise was heard overhead. She recalled the night of the neighborhood pet meeting, the first time Elt had acted strangely. What if she was wrong about Elt tonight? Then she would really make a fool of herself in front of her humans.

Jenny opened the screen door and treaded down the side steps to grab a seat by her friends on a spare step. Bernadette was at her heels, panting slightly with excitement, but rejuvenated and full of energy. Bernadette wasn't surprised to find Oleo present, for Jasmine had informed her of Elt's mission on the spaceship earlier that day. Wanting to convince Trixie that she and Elt were "an item," the Cocker Spaniel cuddled right up against Oleo. Her attention to "Elt" would also help calm any suspicions about Elt's scent or oddities.

Jenny's smile gleamed. She sat up and leaned on the outside wall of her house. She grinned at her friends and waited.

"What is it?" demanded Ralph. "The suspense is too much."

"Yeah, tell us, Jenny," insisted Caroline.

"Well! Remember me telling you that Bernie hasn't been herself lately?" The kids nodded their heads collectively. "Yeah, so my mom and I just returned from Dr. Kelly's office...you know the vet?"

"Was everything okay with Bernie?" questioned Bryan.

"She's fine, but... I mean we have some exciting news," returned Jenny. She paused slightly. Ralph watched his friend's every move. "Bernadette is going to have puppies!"

Except for the birds chirping, there was silence. It took a little time for the news to sink in. "Did you hear me?" laughed Jenny. "My Bernie is going to be a mommy!"

"Ooooooooooh! That's so cool!" squealed Caroline. Bryan bent down and tosseled Bernadette's fur.

"I'm still not sure how it happened," Jenny gleamed. She turned and looked straight at Ralph and Elt. Ralph gulped slightly. He gazed down at his dog. Could it be? Could Elt and Bernadette be parents?

"So who's the daddy?" inquired Bryan.

"I don't know exactly, but I have an idea," teased Jenny. Jenny, Caroline, and Bryan focused their attention on Ralph and Elt. "The funny thing is that my mom and I were talking about allowing Bernie to have one litter of puppies, but I didn't think it would happen this fast."

Bryan reached over and patted the new Elt on the head. "Great job old boy, you're going to be a daddy!" Oleo greeted the boy with a lick on his hand.

"Well, we won't know for sure until the puppies arrive," corrected Jenny.

Ralph still couldn't fathom the possibility of Elt and Bernadette becoming parents. They were so young, but even pups could have puppies at a year old. Sure, he knew that his dog possessed extraordinary abilities, but he had not been aware of Elt's numerous late night excursions while he slept.

So when is Bernadette going to give birth to her puppies?" asked Caroline.

"Dr. Kelly says that a canine's gestation period is around sixty-three days," instructed Jenny.

"Jest a what?" asked Bryan.

"Sorry," giggled Jenny. "It takes about two months for a female dog to…you know…reproduce."

"Have puppies!" exalted Caroline.

"Exactly," laughed Jenny. "Dr. Kelly thinks Bernie is at about thirty-five days."

"So can Bernie still go on walks with us and play?" questioned Bryan.

"Sure," returned Jenny. "The doctor prescribed some vitamins for her. In fact, I wanted Bernie to take a different route today…a shorter one. Can I lead the way?"

The friends and their pets followed Jenny and Bernadette out of her yard. Ralph, who originally worried about Oleo's presence, actually felt better about the situation. Some attention had drifted its way toward his dog, but most of the focus was on Bernadette. Now that the focus was on the Cocker Spaniel, neither Trixie or Seymour uttered a bark or stare during their walk. They seemed unaffected by the replicate's presence.

Jenny proceeded to lead the group in a new direction. Instead of turning right and continuing down Valleydale Drive, Jenny and Bernadette veered left, and then strolled right onto Spring Drive, which was an off-shoot that stemmed out from Valleydale Drive by Sarge's house. The road meandered for about a mile, with houses lined up on either side of the street. Some of the kids that Ralph and Jenny knew lived along Spring Drive.

Ralph and Oleo remained close to Jenny and Bernadette. The Greenlees were not too far behind. Not one of the kids really knew much about that particular part of the neighborhood, but Jenny was intrigued. She had always wanted to walk that way.

"Do you know where this road leads to?" asked Ralph.

"Not sure," responded Jenny. She continued walking past the endless rows of houses lined up on each side of the street.

Suddenly, a series of roaring barks emanated from the third house on the right. A German Shepherd dashed over to the front fence. Both the kids and the pets couldn't quite detect if his barks were friendly or aggressive. The shepherd's tail wagged feverishly. The canine lashed over at the walkers. Trixie returned messages, while Bernadette yelped a couple times herself.

"Rex...Rex...! commanded a voice from behind the German Shepherd. "Calm down boy!"

A boy, possibly about twelve, ran up to the dog. He directed his dog to sit, and then rewarded him with a treat.

"Hey, I know you," said Jenny.

The boy gazed up at the group. "Hey."

Jenny did know the boy, for she had seen him walking by her house on the way home. He wasn't a classmate, for he was older.

"Zach, right?" asked the girl.

"Yeah," returned the older boy.

"Zach Miller," mouthed Ralph to himself as the boy bent down to hug his dog. Zach Miller was indeed older, twelve to be exact. He attended Spring Valley Middle School, which was located on the outer edges of downtown Spring Valley, right next to Spring Valley High School.

Rex was a stalwart, brave, and handsome specimen of a canine. At five years old, the only factor that restrained this mighty beast from becoming a super dog was his age. Coladeus preferred younger specimens, so they would mature and learn how to manage their powers. Rex possessed teeth like a vise, which could tear through a chunk of meat with ease.

To a stranger, Rex was a fierce protector, a guard dog that would not let anyone he didn't recognize pass him without pain. To his family, Rex was a gentle giant, full of love and devotion for his family and their friends.

Zach possessed a certain "coolness" about him, a mature lad of twelve. Nothing seemed to "rattle his cage." He was even-tempered. While running track at the middle school, Zach Miller torched many of the school's records for both short and long distance runs. He was a stellar student and excellent role model for any up-and-coming middle- schooler.

"Will he bite?" asked Bryan as he held Trixie at bay. The poodle, however, wanted to be noticed by the handsome shepherd. She forged ahead of Bryan, twinkled her eyes, and momentarily bowed to Rex. The shepherd noticed the spritely French Poodle, and then fixed his total attention on her. A few odd sniffs Oleo's way produced only slight suspicions, but he quickly averted his attention to Trixie.

"Only on command, or if anyone in my family is in danger," replied Zach. Rex had never really attacked anyone, but Zach wanted to have a little fun with the younger kids.

Oleo was curious, like the other pets, but didn't want to raise any suspicions. He knew what he was supposed to do on his mission—remain calm and stay out of the limelight.

"Can we pet him?" asked Jenny. Bernadette was curious, yet cautious. Jenny edged closer to the fence and slowly placed her hand about a foot away from the German Shepherd's head. Rex obliged, allowing Jenny to pet him. He then licked her hand.

"Anyone else?" asked Zach. Ralph was interested, but keeping Oleo away from Rex was a must. Things were going too good that afternoon. Bryan directed Trixie to remain behind. He eased beside Jenny and offered his hand to Rex. The dog genuinely accepted the boy's sign of affection.

"I gotta go," announced Zach. "Come on boy."

Rex followed his human inside via the garage. The kids gathered themselves, walked a block or two down Spring Drive, and then returned to Jenny's house.

Ralph reported the news of Bernadette's expectancy to his dad. "Wow, that's exciting news," commented Mr. Eltison. Ralph's dad had no clue about Elt's possible connection with Bernadette and the arrival of puppies. "Was this a surprise to Jenny and Ms. Rodgers?"

"Well, kind of," returned Ralph. He explained that Jenny and her mom were planning for Bernadette to have one litter of puppies, but that it had happened sooner than they had imagined.

The first day with Oleo had transpired pretty smoothly, and the kids, along with their pets, had met a new friend. Was Rex going to be a new member of the neighborhood meetings? After dinner and a shower, Ralph played catch with his dog, read part of a book, and then headed to his bedroom for the evening.

Ralph stared at the stars through his window before falling asleep. Somewhere out there was his hero dog, hoping to save the Trianthians.

Although Oleo had made the transition much better this time, the boy still missed the real Elt. He prayed for Elt's safety.

Bernadette fell asleep at the foot of Jenny's bed. She wondered when her partner would return. How she longed to see him, to reveal that soon they would have a family of their own.

Meanwhile, many miles away in deep space, Elt, Sparky, and Klecktonis were engaged in a desperate battle to save the Trianthian race and their very own lives.

CHAPTER 17

ONLY A FAINT GREEN FLICKER of light illuminated the Trianthian control room. Situated in a cavernous bunker below the planet's surface, the "Control Room" as it was referred to (in Trianthian dialect of course,) was where all the controls to the planet's defense and life support systems were located. It was much more than one room, but rather a large complex, hidden to outsiders and to fellow Trianthians, for the protection of the race itself.

In order to find his way through the dark labyrinth of tunnels that led to the secured area of the Control Room, Mogulus held a glowing, miniature wand, composed of a material similar to clear, hard plastic. Everything in the pathway was dark. Kraylen had followed the scientist into the depths, willing and eager to assist in any way he could. "So why are we down here, Mogulus?"

Mogulus didn't answer directly. He stopped at a concealed door, keyed in a code and gave the voice and skin recognition needed for entry. When the door glided open, the two stepped into a quiet defense control center. The genius led Kraylen to a set of eight globes, each about the size of a human basketball. He examined each container swiftly yet carefully, but the light he carried and the light in the globes were faint. "Our defense system has been compromised," stated Mogulus, "I feel that I'm to blame. I should have conducted more experiments. I could have prevented a tragedy like this." He pinched his brow for a moment and then began to finger through a series of commands on some sort of a touch pad situated directly below the array of globes.

"We should all take responsibility, not just you. We were all too confident," claimed Kraylen. "But how is coming down here going to possibly save us from total destruction?"

The master researcher continued to fiddle with the controls. Each globe began to brighten, and then dim, but not nearly as powerfully as when all systems were functioning properly. "Each globe is the master control to one of our isolated defense stations located throughout the planet," explained Mogulus.

"That fact is already known," returned Kraylen in his alien dialect.

"Normal procedure dictates that we power our system equally into each globe," explained the scientist. "But perhaps if we re-direct all of the energy to just one, there would be a surge, potent enough to disrupt the ray which holds us captive." He paused, and then continued more quietly. "And then, just maybe there would be enough energy left for Trianthius I to launch an offensive."

Kraylen was silent for a moment as he recognized the futility, this impossibly thin ray of hope. Then he cleared his throat. "What are our chances that this tactic of yours would be successful?"

Mogulus leveled his tired eyes at Kraylen. "Very minimal."

Just then another door whooshed open and a Trianthian entered. He strode purposefully toward Kraylen and handed him a slate-like chip, about the size of a cookie. The elder frowned as he struggled to decipher the message that was encrypted on the piece.

"What is it?" questioned Mogulus.

"It appears Trianthius I has encountered the Quadrasonian warship," announced Kraylen.

"They don't have enough energy to launch a serious attack." Mogulus shook his head. "If we do this, if we do overload one globe, we could destroy our entire defense system."

"What other choices do we have?" Kraylen's question was rhetorical.

"Yes. Yes," replied the elder heavily. "We must give Coladeus the best possible chance." The scientist prepared a series of program changes and then touched each globe separately. "Here goes nothing. Or everything." Each globe powered down to total darkness, except for one, which brightened considerably, but not to full capacity.

"Anything?" inquired the elder.

Mogulus shrugged his shoulders. "We shall see."

CHAPTER 18

THE CABIN WAS DARK. THE Trianthian captain winced as he gazed around an empty room. His body ached, liked it had never ached before. He didn't know what to expect. How was he going to surrender Trianthius I?

Suddenly, a yellowish head appeared, and then a second. To Coladeus, they appeared to be sentries, ordered to retrieve him. A chamber door opened. One of the guardsman motioned for the Trianthian to exit the chamber. No words were spoken. Coladeus rose and exited slowly.

The captain watched the two guards glide ahead of him, almost like ghosts. Were these Quadrasones real, or just specters of evil? Scores of thoughts roamed through Coladeus's troubled mind. He was too weak to fight the enemy. "How can I save Trianthius I?" the leader agonized to himself.

Coladeus was used to the darkness inside his own ship, but the absence of light on the Quadrasonian ship was thick and ominous. The walls and the doors resembled a massive castle dungeon.

The three stepped onto a floating platform, its neon blue hue barely visible in the close darkness that surrounded them. The platform rose slowly upwards in the cavernous room. There were no real levels or floors but they passed by other floating transports as they traveled. The group continued to climb higher and higher, and then suddenly stopped. The platform edged forward slightly. Coladeus glanced downward. All he could see were tiny yellow dots, quite possibly working Quadrasones way below, mingling about in various directions. A sudden banging of metal focused Coladeus on things ahead rather than below. A humongous door pivoted inward, revealing the breathtaking Quadrasonian bridge; the heart of the enemy ship.

Coladeus was helpless. There was nowhere to run, nowhere to hide. He hoped to convince his captors to spare his crew and ship, but he knew that proposal would be nearly impossible. In the middle of the room sat Zemak, hovering in front of the screen. There in the picture lie Trianthius I, motionless.

For one of the first times in his long life, Coladeus was frightened, not for himself, but for his crew and the Trianthians struggling for their lives on his planet. The encounter with Zemak was the closest he'd ever been to a Quadrasone, and they were scary creatures. In the back of his mind, Coladeus knew there was one thin hope, but would it happen in time?

The guards ushered Coladeus closer to their leader. He stood still in front of Zemak's angry stare while the two sentries remained in the background. Coladeus reached into his pouch for his distransulator, but then realized that his device didn't translate their dialect. Secondly, he knew communication would differ since Quadrasones had no mouths.

Zemak motioned and a crewmate rushed over to Coladeus. The yellow figure adhered a small, olive-colored device onto Coladeus's uniform lapel. Zemak's eyes burned like fiery daggers right through the weakened Trianthian. There was so much hatred and anger. Coladeus sensed it. Zemak turned his attention back to the holographic image and paused momentarily.

"I trust you can hear me clearly," announced Zemak through the aid of the transmitter Coladeus wore on his lapel. The Quadrasone continued to stare at the image, his back turned away from the captain. Coladeus paused.

"Just speak into the unit which my associate applied to your uniform," instructed Zemak. He continued to disrespect his counterpart by ignoring his presence and staring at his conquest.

"Why have you committed this atrocious attack on our planet?" Coladeus spoke with more command than he felt.

Zemak didn't respond. He watched the picture contentedly.

"What act of violence or negligence have we committed to warrant such a seizure of our planet's natural resources?" Coladeus demanded.

In an instant, Zemak thrust backwards, and then lunged at Coladeus, stopping only inches from his adversary. Those eyes. "What I *wanted* you to ask me was how were we able to infiltrate your sophisticated forcefield and drain your planet of all of its power?" Zemak's anger made room for a bit of pride.

Coladeus remained quiet.

"I see," smirked the Quadrasonian. "I'm sure you want to know."

Zemak circled Coladeus via his floating chair. "For many of your duraceps as you call them, our scientists have been conducting countless experiments. Our biggest question was what gives your planet's crystals their power?" Zemak continued. "We could never pinpoint the exact weakness. But while on a planet that we...let's say encountered... our troops gathered resources from the planet and forwarded them to our top researchers. Our scientists discovered something truly amazing... The properties from that planet not only weakened the Trianthian crystals, they eventually destroyed them!"

Coladeus watched Zemak's eyes protrude, as if they were going to bulge right out of their sockets. "So while your miniscule armada has been chasing us here and there, we've been experimenting, perfecting the most powerful laser in the universe," rambled Zemak through his mind-speak. Now we're destroying your pitiful Trianthian crystals and your citizens for good."

Coladeus was speechless. He had yearned to know, and now he really got to meet the foe that had defeated him. But there was no antidote, and so far no rescue. Coladeus had to buy time, for he knew that his time was short. "I'd like to discuss the surrender of my crew," stated Coladeus as he spoke into the tiny transmitter. "I want to be assured that no harm will come to them."

Zemak turned away, and then once again zoomed over to his counterpart. "We will make no allowances for surrender or survival."

"But I came here to surrender, in order to save my crew," pleaded the Trianthian.

"I will guarantee this," motioned the Quadrasonian. "Their demise will be quick and painless. One moment they will be here, the next, gone."

A crewmember handed Zemak a small gadget, about the size of a matchbox. The box displayed a red button on the top.

"You know what this is?" asked Zemak.

Coladeus had a notion, but decided to remain silent.

"This device is a miniature version of what is annihilating your world, and I plan to use it on you," scorned Zemak.

"What makes your species so evil?" Coladeus hated feeling so defeated.

If he owned a mouth, Zemak would have grinned. "Because we were meant to be. You Trianthians have been in our way, duracep after duracep as you name your period in time. Time to say goodbye, foe."

And with that last threat, Zemak directed the device at Coladeus and pushed the red button. The mechanism fired a stream of rays at the Trianthian leader, crippling him. Coladeus struggled to remain on his feet, but after the third round of beams, the captain slumped and tumbled to the ground. His body remained motionless.

Zemak released his clawed hold on the red button. He waved for a crewmate to check on Coladeus. As the Quadrasone glided over to Coladeus's lifeless body, in an instant, the Trianthian leader disappeared into thin air.

"What?" seethed Zemak as he rushed over to the spot from which Coladeus had just vanished. The rest of the crew searched the bridge; Coladeus was gone.

An alarm sounded, a very harsh-sounding drone, sure to rattle eardrums. Zemak turned around. "It can't be," he cried.

The helmsman, who guided the warship, raised his head from his visual screen. "It is confirmed! Our shields are down!"

A combination of shock and disbelief overcame what was supposed to be a victorious moment for the Quadrasones. A crushing blow slammed the Quadrasonian warship. They were under attack! Another barrage of firepower walloped the bridge. Fires began to erupt all over the ship.

Zemak rushed over to his holographic screen. The picture was sketchy, but all that could be seen were the two disabled Trianthian vessels floating aimlessly in space. Then it appeared out of nowhere: A ship almost twice the size of the warship whizzed by and turned around. It was heading for its final assault!

CHAPTER 19

"DUDE, WHAT ARE YOU DOING up there?" inquired Sparky.

Elt probed an area of the spaceship's ceiling. It was much easier to fly to his destination, for the lack of gravity enabled the super dog to soar effortlessly. Sparky watched inquisitively from his perch beside the alien Klecktonis. He adjusted his mask; now that the ship was in deep space, there was a lack of oxygen. Evidently, Klecktonis's ship wasn't equipped with the proper oxygen levels necessary to provide trouble-free breathing for the canines.

"I know I heard something," quipped Elt. He began to sniff around, but the mask made the task too difficult to discern any abnormalities.

"What's going on up there?" asked Sparky once again.

"I thought I heard something, the same type of sound when we were on the time transport machine," returned Elt.

"What are you blabbering about?" Sparky jumped off his perch and glided over to his friend. He, of course, had no knowledge about Elt's time machine adventure. He didn't understand Elt's correlation between the time machine and the spaceship. Elt sensed that something

84

indeed wasn't right. Klecktonis turned around to catch a glimpse of their conversation.

"There it is! I told you," pointed Elt. A crack emerged, about a half inch in depth, and increasing in length by the seconds.

"Klecky baby, shine some beamage over here," barked Sparky.

The alien, who was now deeply concerned about the two canines' concerns, showered a stream of light across the ship to illuminate the growing crack. Then she extinguished the light, turned around, and began to paw at several buttons on her console. A small microphone and speaker lowered itself from the hatch above her. The alien spoke into the microphone, perhaps leaving some sort of distress signal to whoever was out there. Who would be out there in deep space? A scratchy sound resonated from the speaker, with a mixture of whistles and beeps.

"What do we do?" asked Elt. The dogs didn't even know where they were going. They didn't even know if Klecktonis knew where they were going.

Sparky scanned the situation. The seam continued to widen, crumbling to the pressure of the trip into deep space. Sparky spotted several areas in the ceiling that resembled hooks or handles.

"Do you see any rope?" asked the retriever. The dogs both knew what rope was, for they had both played tug-of-war with their humans. The rope they required would have to be lengthy.

Elt leaped away and zoomed from place to place, area to hidden area. Hanging on a wall nearby was a nylon-like material. "I think this will do." Elt clenched onto the rope and blasted over to Sparky. The Golden Retriever snagged one end of the rope and pulled.

"Bite right here," instructed Sparky. Elt chomped into the rope and it easily snapped.

"Are you following what I'm thinking?" questioned Sparky.

"I think so," followed Elt. "We wrap rope up here and there..."

"And hold on tight until..." Sparky blinked. "We just hold on tight."

Elt lunged upward and laced his rope through the hook-and-eye on one side of the crack. Sparky followed suit and accomplished the same task on the other side. The two super dogs snatched both of the ends of their ropes and tugged. If their plan worked, the ship would hold together. If they failed, the crack would open further, and all three would likely be sucked out into deep space.

The cracking stopped momentarily as the two pulled with all their might; their combined strength was superior, but for how long? Even superheroes have limits. Several hours passed. Klecktonis's messages ceased for a period of time, but then the beeping and whistling started to increase again. The two warriors fed off each other, with one dog easing just a little to conserve energy, relying on the other for support. Then they would change up.

"Klecky, I'm not sure how much longer we can hold on," barked Sparky as he struggled to maintain his grip on the rope. The thread on the rope was worn and about to break apart. Elt's power had never been tested for this length of time. He was growing weaker, with only pure adrenaline maintaining his strength. It seemed that the strength of their stones hadn't yet deteriorated due to the lack of power on Trianthius. It was a good thing. Elt's nylon, too, was about to snap.

The devastation to the ship, although slowed by Elt's and Sparky's quick-thinking heroism, had hindered the ship's speed and direction. The alien was finding it difficult to steer her ship in the appropriate direction.

And then Sparky's rope snapped. The retriever fell backwards and crashed into the wall of the spaceship. The tear in the ceiling instantly widened. Elt struggled to maintain his end, but the suction from the outside dragged both him and Sparky toward the break in the ceiling. If they were forced out into space, even with their exceptional strength and speed, the two would only last as long as the miniscule oxygen supply they carried on their backs. With no oxygen, the dogs would perish in minutes.

Various pieces of equipment flew out of the ship as the crack widened even further. A hole large enough for two canines splintered the ceiling of the ship. Elt held on for dear life, securing himself to some shelving attached to the ship's floor. His oxygen mask flew off. Sparky was somewhere in the distance, for Elt could hear him barking.

"Breathe, breathe," Elt thought to himself, but air was desperately low. Klecktonis bravely commandeered the ship to its bitter end, hanging on to the ship's steering mechanism. In his last moment of consciousness, Elt saw something bright white come into view via the crack overhead, like the ship had been swallowed by a large, white whale. Was this the end? Elt was so young. Would he ever see Ralph again? His home? Bernadette?

Elt closed his eyes...

CHAPTER 20

DARKNESS BECAME LIGHT.....

The super dog opened his bleary eyes. Everything was white. He groggily recalled the bright light as he was phasing out. His eyes fell onto the fifteen foot-wide opening of the ship's ceiling. "Where am I?" he thought.

"You all right buddy?" asked a familiar voice. "We almost lost you there." Sparky emerged into view. He sniffed Elt for a few seconds and raised his head. "He's good!" Sparky raised his right paw up in the air.

Elt attempted to snap out of the trance he felt he was in. Either he was experiencing the weirdest dream, or something truly miraculous had occurred. He looked up once again. Sparky was right beside him. Above, at the site of the huge gap in the ship, stood Kelcktonis; her stance valiant and vigilant. "You ready to get outta here?" asked Sparky. Elt nodded.

"You're gonna have to fly out," continued Sparky. He jetted upwards. Elt sat up, shook off a chill, and then without hesitation, followed his friend, past Klecktonis. The alien then jumped off the top of the ship and landed impressively on her feet.

Elt was still bewildered. The broken ship was stationary, resting in some type of cargo area, completely white. He was on board a huge spaceship, but whose? "You see old Klecky, well she signaled for help," informed Sparky. "And Crazy Legs and the behemoth over there, rescued us just in time. I thought I was a goner for sure."

Elt glanced over and saw Myotaur and Widenmauer, the two space heroes that had teamed up with them on the space mission to Titan. Klecktonis joined the group of aliens, pointing to other areas of her ship that had sustained damages during her voyage from Earth.

Elt thought his eyes were playing tricks on him. There were three other Widenmauer-type creatures in the room, six-legged freaks running and crawling around everywhere. The scene resembled a B-rated science-fiction movie. Elt watched with amazement as the beings scurried about, transferring from task to task with both ease and efficiency. There were no webs present in the cargo area; the room was clean.

"Relax, you're not the only one seeing a bunch of crazy legs," assured Sparky.

"What's going on?" worried Elt.

"Here's the deal," assured the retriever. "Laser eyes, well she called the other two, and crazy legs, he has this gigantor space ship. They rescued us in the nick of time. And well, there's a whole crew of these spider things, and I'm not sure which one ate the bug." Sparky was referring to the mission to Titan, when Widenmauer wrapped and devoured his catered meal from the Trianthians. "Anyway," continued Sparky, "we're on our way to kick some Quadrasone butt. This ship is massive!"

Elt rose and began to walk around. The ordeal on Klectonis' ship had drained him. His legs were still queasy, but he could at last feel his strength returning. "Dude, let's go see what they've got in their fridge," suggested Sparky. "I'm hungrier than a bullfrog in a fly factory!"

Elt agreed. The canines trekked through the cargo area, past the tattered spaceship and discovered a set of doors that led to a dark corridor, fluttering with tangled webs. The dogs had to carefully weave their way through the maze of sticky fibers lining the hallway. "Maybe this wasn't a good idea after all," frowned Elt.

The dogs noticed an eerie, orange light up ahead. As they drew closer, the heroes were surprised by the presence of a sentry standing by a huge, wooden door. The orange beam resembled fire, but emitted no heat or smoke. The door slowly opened, creaking its way to a full stop. A couple of creatures exited, and then one entered. The two watched from about ten feet away as more beings entered and exited the door. Some characters resembled the six-legged species, others didn't.

"Must be some kind of garbage factory, or maybe a cafeteria." commented Sparky. The retriever began to lick his chops, imagining what tasty treats might be hiding behind the guarded door. "Let's go for it dude."

Elt walked side-by-side with his friend. They approached the door together. The sentry appeared to be looking forward, but with spider-like eyes, who could tell? The creature made no movements toward the canines. Elt figured an explanation would be in order, but when the guard continued to stare straight ahead, the dogs forged on and opened the door.

The room was vast; about a couple football fields in length and thirty feet in height. Artificial light illuminated the area. The room resembled a jungle or rainforest, for there were trees, grass, wild flowers, and the sound of running water. A drone-like noise buzzed about, adding to the creepiness of this strange, new place.

Elt edged his way in first. He sniffed his surroundings. The door closed, and then moments later, opened again, and two of the spidery creatures entered. They passed by the dogs and proceeded to climb up a couple of nearby trees and disappear.

"This place is a little creepy'" snipped Elt.

"Is this what I think it is?" murmured Sparky.

"It's like a giant backyard," whispered Elt. "What do you think it is?"

A thrashing noise emanated from the trees above them; a squealing sound in fact. Leaves scattered about and fell harmlessly to the ground. Then there was just the drone and the running of possibly a waterfall.

"This is no 'caferteria,'" quipped Sparky.

"You mean they hunt for their food?" returned Elt.

Sparky pointed. "Looky up there." Elt squinted to pinpoint the desired location. Nestled about twenty feet in the air, dangling from a tree limb, was one of the arachnids. It was spinning its prey; a red beetle-like being about a foot long. The bug struggled to free itself, but it wasn't going to escape. There was another rustling in the jungle, about thirty feet away.

"Well, let's see if there's anything for us in here," Sparky decided. "I have a feeling unless you want bugs or worms, the menu is going to be limited."

Elt sniffed ahead. "First things first, I need to take care of business."

"Me too," agreed Sparky. The two scattered momentarily, but not too far away. It had been a long trip without a bathroom break.

Once back together, Elt and Sparky searched diligently through the make-believe rainforest configured in the middle of Weidenmauer's spaceship. The dogs were indeed grateful for the rescue, but now hunger took over, and they weren't used to hunting for their food. Discouragement and frustration befuddled them.

The two discovered slithering snakes, grub worms hiding under rocks, lizards, and some creatures that they had never encountered before. "I'd prefer a vending machine right now," whispered Sparky.

Elt had no clue what a vending machine was. Sparky had watched his human drop something, money, into the slot, and packaged food was there for their consumption. "Uh, I'd wouldn't mind some stuff that my human feeds me right now." Elt gathered one last set of whiffs. "Time to get a better view of this place."

Elt blasted off first, upwards toward the tops of the trees. Sparky soared toward the tree-tops. Elt pointed to a waterfall below, surrounded by rocks, trees, and flowers. The canines spiraled downwards and landed. They both sniffed around. There seemed to be no dangers. "Dude, we can hunt, just not like those guys," reasoned Sparky. "We are gifted with these amazing talents, surely we can hunt us down some grub."

"I don't see any birds," commented Elt. "What did you have in mind?"

Sparky scanned the forest. "Not even a squirrel or rabbit. I never ate one of those before, but when you're hungry, you're hungry." And then

Sparky spotted something. He dashed over to the water. There was an abundance of fish, swimming in the stream. "I'm neither a cat nor a bear, but I can do this." He jumped into the stream.

"Not sure if I've ever had one of these before," grimaced Elt. "Probably not." Elt sucked in a breath, then leaped past Sparky and plunged into the water. Although the canines were quick, the fish were speedier. Sparky was determined, Elt a little more hesitant.

"Come on you," grunted Sparky. "Don't you want to be fish fillet for Sparky today?" The fish thrashed about, but patience paid off. Sparky whisked down and nabbed one close to a foot long. Elt was amazed. He watched his friend walk back to land with the prize in his mouth. Then suddenly, Sparky tossed the fish back into the water.

"What's up?" inquired Elt.

"I'm thinking," started Sparky. "What if these fish are like not meant for our bodies? What if they're 'poisoneeous'?"

Elt thought for a second or two. "Good point."

Right then, a deafening sound blared throughout the forest. Its ear-dropping blare was a warning, but for what? Within seconds, about a dozen creatures, some with six legs, and some without, scurried out of their hiding places and headed for the entrance.

"Let's see what's going on," Sparky suggested.

Elt agreed. The two jetted upward once again and landed about ten feet in front of the door, startling the crowd of beings that were about to exit. Elt looked all around. "Where do we go?"

Sparky watched as a group of six-leggers exited and then darted right. "Let's follow them!"

Even with their above-average speeds, the canines were challenged, for six leggers moved faster than two or four legs could. Another dozen creatures migrated to an opening, a spacious, brighter room that resembled the cargo landing arena. The beings consisted mainly of arachnids, but the pooches spotted Klecktonis and Myotaur standing in a disorganized line.

"Looks like they're lining up for something, but what?" asked Elt.

"Let's go check it out."

As the two drew closer, they noticed a familiar sight. Situated in the middle of the staging area were transport modules, very similar to the

Trianthian models. The arachnids in line were being fitted with special masks; others received inoculations, presumably to counteract whatever climate they were about to encounter.

Thunderous echoes suddenly shook the ship, as if it were laying an assault of significant magnitude. A screeching noise alerted everyone in the room. A giant screen materialized out of thin air, and the group could witness what the commotion was all about. The picture depicted the Quadrasonian ship under an attack from an array of web-like explosives, causing it to slowly retreat. In the distance, both Trianthian ships floated lifelessly in space. Also in the background lie Trianthius itself, with little more than a dim, dull glow of listless light. Its triangular perimeter was barely visible.

"We're firing something crazy good at those pointy heads!" rejoiced Sparky.

"He did have a plan," smiled Elt.

"What?"

"It all makes sense now," continued Elt. "She picks us up on Earth. Then we join this space transporter. The body movers over there, they're from Coladeus. He knew they were under attack from the pointy heads. This was all his plan. He knew he needed help, from all of us."

Sparky gazed at the screen. "I hope we arrived in time, partner."

Coladeus had miraculously managed to organize this rescue mission in addition to aiding Ralph, Elt, and the time travelers twenty-five years into Spring Valley's future. Between discovering the Quadrasones on Titan and assisting the time travelers, Coladeus suspected that Trianthius was under attack. He had to react…and fast. The weaknesses he and his crew had experienced were the clincher to his assumptions.

Weidenmauer's race wasn't well known, therefore there was no term labelling them such as humans, Trianthians, or Quadrasones. All that was obvious was that they resembled spiders, but only bore six legs instead of eight. Their race was also obviously advanced in technology, enough to possess a thoroughbred-like spaceship strong enough to disrupt a warship the size of the Quadrasones'.

But how did this imposing spaceship "sneak up" undetected on the enemy? The arachnid scientists developed a method based on their own hunting skills. The ship, although white on the exterior, was able to camouflage itself to its surroundings in order to successfully hunt its prey. So in deep space, Widenmauer's ship was able to disguise itself as deep space. Their anatomies gave off no heat, and they extinguished all communications way in advance of their approach to the warship. By the time Coladeus's body disappeared from the Quadrasonian's vessel, the ship was in easy firing range of its specially designed web-like rays that provided damaging blows to the enemy.

As Weidenmauer's ship continued to pummel the Quadrasonian warship, a disturbance arose near the transport modules. Several arachnids began to board the transport modules. "I think those dudes are heading for the transport," blurted Sparky. "I want in." He surged forward.

A discussion arose between the two arachnids stationed at the module controls and Weidenmauer. Klecktonis and Myotaur dashed past several other arachnids and joined the three. In a matter of seconds, communications were exchanged, and the beings that had boarded the modules were ordered to leave. The crowd around the transports backed away. "What's going on now?" asked Elt.

Sparky stopped moving and checked out the scene. "Let's edge in closer."

All of a sudden, the room fell silent. There were no more screeches; no more booms or sirens. Within seconds, the lights on the transport modules began to blink. A body materialized in front of them. The body was still, lying on the floor of the tube-like container, motionless.

Myotaur and Klecktonis rushed over. The blue behemoth, Myotaur, picked up the body and set it on a nearby floating table. It was the Trianthian...Coladeus. He lay completely still.

"Oh no," grimaced Elt. "It can't be."

Sparky remained silent. The concerned canines crept closer to the body. They whiffed and sniffed for a moment, and then stared at each other. Tears began to stream out of Sparky's eyes. Elt began to sob, also. Klecktonis laid her hand on the back of Elt's scruff. She too was in mourning of a friend and leader.

Widenmauer exchanged some communications with Myotaur and Klecktonis. Even though their species differed, it seemed to Elt and Sparky that the heroes understood each other. Klecktonis streaked off, out of the room, her long strides gliding effortlessly through the corridors. The alien scaled the outside of her ship, dropped inside her old vessel, reached for her knapsack, and then selected a few items to place in the bag. She leaped back down, and raced back to meet her comrades.

Unbeknownst to the alien, the little stowaway, which had fluttered its way on board when the ship blasted off from Earth, had somehow survived the treacherous voyage. It latched on to Klecktonis's knapsack and crept its way inside.

The focus of the group in the staging area had shifted from Coladeus's body to the battle on the big screen. The Quadrasonian warship, being pummeled by the massive, stronger vessel, released its paralyzing ray on Trianthius and its armada. The warship attempted to retaliate against Widenmauer's ship, but was unsuccessful, for Widenmauer's craft was zoning in on its final assault. Instead, the enemy vessel turned and blasted off in retreat. The whole assembly in the staging area shrieked and cheered. The battle, it appeared, was over.

The aggressor didn't pursue the weakened enemy warship. A decision had been made; pay respects to a great leader and aid a dying planet.

Myotaur motioned for the two canines. He picked up the Trianthian's body and walked into one of the modules. Elt and Sparky realized what was next. They stepped into their own individual cylinders. Widenmauer waited, followed by Klecktonis, who had just returned from her ship.

Masks were fitted on the travelers, for the planet's oxygen levels couldn't be verified as sufficient for the canines. It wasn't known what element was needed for Myotaur's survival, but a mask was applied to him as well. Within seconds, the blue giant and the canines vanished, hoping to discover some sort of life left on Trianthius.

CHAPTER 21

ELT'S HEART RACED. HE HAD traveled in one of the modules before, so that wasn't the reason for his anxiety. His friend, his mentor, lie motionless in the transporter next to him. What would the space heroes do without their leader? Elt had very few memories about his mother and father. He did though, belong to a family: Ralph and Mr. Eltison. But Coladeus was more than a friend. He was almost like a father. Elt couldn't believe the Trianthian had perished.

In less than thirty seconds, Elt materialized onto the planet's surface; flat rocks near a stretch of trees, hills, and a river. Elt, Sparky, and Myotaur scanned the area before them. Trianthius usually remained pretty dark, with the glow from the Trianthian crystals brightening the planet. Now one could see the devastation caused by the Quadrasonian assault. Flowers and grass were burnt and limp. The air was stagnant. Scores of leaves had fallen to the ground. The once vibrant river only trickled. The planet's vibrant glow was lost and Trianthius remained at an uncomfortable dusk.

Widenmauer and Klecktonis appeared. The heroes waited. Within a short period of time, a young Trianthian crept out from a hidden door embedded in a wall of stone. The Trianthian noticed Coladeus, rushed over, touched the captain's forehead, and then motioned for the others to follow.

"I can't believe Coladeus is gone," murmured Elt.

Sparky just shook his head in disbelief. "You and me both brother."

As they followed the Trianthian through the stone door into the darkness, Elt felt like he was descending, even though there were no stairs. Faint light emanating from wall sconces enabled the crew to travel through the darkness. Klecktonis flipped her mask off and turned her eyes on. Myotaur continued to carry the captain's body.

They finally reached a door, which opened automatically. Once inside, the space heroes were greeted by members of the Trianthian council, seated in a semi-circle in a faintly-lit room. Klecktonis shined her specs on the council. They grimaced, for the light hurt their eyes. They too were still very weak and exhausted from the battle. Kraylen and Mogulus were seated with the rest of the members of the council.

The blue giant quietly laid the body on a platform in front of the group. Elt and Sparky remained closely behind the others. The room was silent. Mogulus was the first to rise and visit Coladeus. He bent down and placed one of his four-fingered hands on the body. The scientist shook his head.

"So he is really gone..?" asked Sparky.

Mogulus reached for his distranslator and adjusted the language to canine-speak. "It's hard to tell. Trianthians possess different anatomies than those of humans or canines. We don't have a heart that pumps blood to all the parts of our body. We survive off the power generated by our planet."

"So you mean you never really die?" inquired Elt.

"Oh, we can perish," returned Mogulus. "If we remain this low on re-generation and don't re-energize after a certain period of time, we will cease to exist."

"So what can we do to save him?" offered Elt.

"Well," started Mogulus, "the good news is that the Quadrasones are gone for now, which means we are no longer under the grip of their dreadful ray. The bad news is that our planet is basically paralyzed. We will require a miracle not only to save Coladeus's life, but to save all of us."

Widenmauer, Myotaur, and Klecktonis couldn't decipher canine-speak, but they fully understood the theme of the discussion. They understood that not only was their friend in a world of hurt; the planet and its inhabitants would wither to nothing soon.

"We can't just stand here and allow the boss to die…let you all die," Sparky stated firmly.

"Perhaps we can form a search party…see if there are any resources we could use," chimed Kraylen, who had been sitting quietly at the conference table.

"Perhaps," replied Mogulus. He switched his distransulator in order to speak to Widenmauer. "Has your crew boarded Trianthius I and II?" The arachnid nodded, speaking in an almost chirp-like manner, but not as high pitched as Klecktonis.

"Yes, I think we should send a team to tour the planet's surface and survey the damage," concluded the scientist. Although not a true officer, Mogulus was an elder and was well respected. There had been times in the planet's history when he had taken charge in difficult situations. This was one more of those times.

Something caught the corner of the scientist's eye. A faint but obvious flicker of light emanating from Klecktonis's knapsack partially illuminated an area in the room. The tiny creature, the stowaway, crept out of the alien's bag, intent on investigating its surroundings.

"What we require is a source of energy…our energy," continued Mogulus. He rose and bent over to closely examine the crawler attached to the alien's bag. "I wonder where this originated." He adjusted his language device and asked the canines.

Elt and Sparky attempted to sniff the small creature through their masks. Elt recognized its glowing feature. "I think it lives in my backyard. It blinks on and off when it's dark outside."

Mogulus examined the being closely. He reached for his specs, which were situated on the top of his head, and positioned them over his eyes. "I recognize this amazing creature. I have studied its properties for duraceps. *Lampyridae* is its earthly science name I believe." Mogulus turned to face the space heroes. "The firefly, as humans call it. Its body's properties resemble that of Trianthians…the way it illuminates. That it survived through this difficult journey is truly a miracle."

Kraylen had been following the scientist's conversation. He adjusted his language device. "Are you thinking what I'm thinking?"

Mogulus nodded. "Its properties…the light it produces is very similar to our Trianthian crystals. Biolumenescence is the human term I recall."

"So you're intimating that this little 'firefly' as you name it can possibly save our species?" questioned Kraylen.

"Well, if it is strong enough to withstand the initial transformation…" mused the scientist.

Sparky's tail began to wag, for he sensed a glimmer of hope. Could this lone firefly, the stowaway from Earth, save Trianthius? It was incredible!

"It's our only hope," reflected Kraylen. "It may be the miracle we need."

Mogulus nodded. "Follow me," he directed. The inventor struggled to keep his balance, but mustered all of his inner strength to move onward. He collected the firefly carefully and cupped the insect in his hand.

Elt and Sparky trailed the scientist first, followed by the three space heroes and Kraylen. Myotaur once again was in charge of gathering Coladeus. Mogulus ventured about two hundred yards down a dark corridor until he slumped, exhausted from the strenuous walk. Widenmauer moved forward, clung onto Mogulus's cloak with one of his legs, and then fully supported the researcher with another leg, utilizing his other four legs to walk.

Just before entering the outside world of Trianthius, Mogulus directed the group to stop at the last door on the right. They had reached the scientist's private laboratory, where he and Kraylen had been recently reviewing the scrolls. Mogulus dismounted stiffly off of the arachnid, opened the laboratory door, and reached for a small canister, placing the firefly gently into the cup.

"Grab one of those please," requested Mogulus, referring to a Trianthian crystal that was discarded in a pile on one of the lab tables.

Elt fetched the crystal and served it to the scientist. Since he was the inventor of the regeneration chamber, Mogulus was privileged to have one of his own machines in his lab. There were scores of chambers located throughout the planet, both above and below ground.

Mogulus placed the firefly's canister in the charging chamber, and then centered the crystal in the middle of the receiving portion of the contraption. Let's hope we have enough power in this little firefly to accomplish this."

Elt watched in anticipation, not quite sure of what was happening. "What's he doing with my backyard bug?"

Sparky scanned the room nervously. "Dude, I think that little bug is going to power-up this place."

Mogulus pushed a series of buttons. Astonishingly, the regeneration chamber operated, transferring bioluminescence from the firefly to the rock. After a few more moments, the machine's cycle ended. "We need you just one more time, little firefly."

Mogulus reached for the crystal and inserted a new one inside. He inspected the re-energized crystal and smiled in near disbelief. "Success!" He removed the firefly momentarily, and replaced the canister with the newly charged crystal. He repeated the steps. Moments later, a second stone was energized, this time from the strength of the newly formed crystal.

Kraylen gazed at the lifeless body still stretched across Myotaur's arms. "Can we…?"

Mogulus nodded. "If this is successful, we must make haste and deliver crystals to the ships. We have many lives to save."

Myotaur placed Coladeus's body inside the receiving chamber, and then placed the firefly back in its original place. It was time to see if Coladeus could be brought back to life.

No one breathed. Everyone's eyes were glued to the chamber. Widenmauer, in a fit of nervous energy, climbed above the machine and spun himself a web.

Mogulus threw the switch. Moments later, the machine finished its cycle. Mogulus gulped, and then slowly opened the door.

CHAPTER 22

THE TABBY CAT JUMPED OFF her perch and landed in the Greenlee's yard. Where was Seymour? She couldn't locate Trixie. Where was everyone? She had to tell someone!

Jasmine dashed across the street. It had been mid-morning when the news had been related to the tabby cat. Jasmine knew that there was something going on with her friend, but now it all made sense. She was in luck. Juan had just circled the yard. He knew who she was, so there was no need for a bark. Jasmine tight-roped the top of his fence and then leaped down in front of the Chihuahua.

"Buenas Dias Seniorita," greeted Juan.

Jasmine waltzed around Juan, her joy eeking out from every hair in her slender body.

"Am I missing something?" squinted Juan. "It is lovely to see you so content this morning."

"It is a glorious day Juan," gleamed Jasmine. "Can you even guess why I am so elated?"

Juan thought for a moment. "Um, your human switched to a new cat litter?"

"No Silly, I'm an outdoor feline. I go where I go. No, it's some really awesome news about someone we know very close to us, and it's grand, so grand!"

Juan was befuddled. Never had he witnessed his feline companion so joyous and gleeful. "Okay okay, que pasa already?"

Jasmine was radiant. "I am going to be an aunt...well kind of I guess."

"Now I'm even more confused." Juan started to scratch at his neck.

"Bernadette and Elt...they're going to have puppies!" shrieked Jasmine.

"Puppies? Puppies?" Juan paced around a small tree. "She can be a madre already?"

"Si! Si!" laughed Jasmine. After a few minutes of rejoicing, it was time for Jasmine to move on and inform the next neighborhood pet.

"Can I be 'Uncle Juan'?" the Chihuahua called out as Jasmine trekked over to Sarge's house.

"I'm sure Bernadette won't mind," she answered.

The Boxer was slumbering as usual in his doghouse, and it required a select number of high-pitched meows to wake the sleeping beast. "What puppies?" gawked Sarge. "They're still little whippersnappers themselves." Sarge paced nervously in front of his doghouse. "How did you...?"

"She told me this morning," replied Jasmine. "She hadn't been feeling like herself lately. I knew something was up. She wanted to tell Elt first, but couldn't wait any longer."

Sarge scratched his head momentarily. "Wait... she could tell Elt anytime. I just saw him a day or two ago. He was walking with the others, you know with Mr. and Mrs. Fancy Pants over there." Sarge was referring to Trixie and Seymour of course.

Sarge was correct in his assumption, but he didn't realize that the Elt he witnessed was a replicate. Some things were better left unsaid, without explanation, but Jasmine loved to toy with the Boxer. "Oh well, you know, that really wasn't Elt you saw walking," taunted Jasmine as she began to walk away. "It's an alien named Oleo from outer space. That's where Elt is right now."

"Outer space? What in tarnation are you talking about?" Sarge shook his boggled head. "I guess we should call a meeting...Is there going to be a puppy shower or something?" Sarge continued to pace back and forth. "That might make me an uncle or something," he mumbled to himself. Then he noticed that Jasmine was now out of his yard. "Wait a darn minute, what do you mean an alien?" he hollered.

"And by the way, we have a new member we need to invite to our next meeting," meowed Jasmine from a distance. "His name is Rex!"

"Rex?...Who's Rex?...Who's Oreo?" Sarge muttered loudly to himself and continued his frantic pace, expanding his perimeter to the back side of his house.

The next appointment on Jasmine's list was Old Max. She had to wait on him for an extended period of time, but the little break afforded her a "cat nap" under Mrs. Petrie's covered porch. It was close to noon when the old Sheepdog ventured out of his air-conditioned palace to sniff some air and take care of his business.

"Puppies huh? That's wonderful news." Max yawned and stretched. "There's never a dull moment around here since those two young'uns joined our neighborhood."

Jasmine next found Chin in meditation but whispered the news to him. "Young flowers produce many young petals," was the Chow-Chow's typically cryptic response, but at least he was awake and alert.

Jasmine spotted the Greenlee pets as she left Chin's doghouse. Seymour pounced on a grasshopper while Trixie pranced around the yard. "Puppies? You mean we're going to be subject to a bunch of little rugrats wailing about?" said Seymour with disdain. "Well, I'm sure they'll be adorable, provided that her humans don't get the undesirable notion of keeping them all."

"I do declare, puppies at such a young age," quipped Trixie. There was a hint of jealously, for she still had hoped for Elt's attentions. "I wonder how those young sprites will affect her petite figure?" Trixie pranced away from Seymour and Jasmine. Deep down she was upset, almost jealous of the news, but her pride would never let it be known.

"One more character to rouse," summarized Jasmine as she leaped over the Greenlee's fence. Her final destination: the Doberman Pinscher. But another nap ensued on Mr. Dawkins's front porch before Prince surfaced for his perimeter walk.

"You are forbidden to sleep here," snubbed Prince as he snuck up on the sleeping tabby. The day's rigorous schedule had fatigued her, but she knew she was in no danger with the Doberman's daunting presence. "Puppies. I must say they're going to be ugly mutts," smirked Prince. "Only pure breeds like myself warrant authenticity. Mutts unfortunately get cast aside, poor creatures."

Jasmine's mouth dropped. "Say what? You're kidding, right?"

Prince rolled his eyes. "Next time I confront Miss Bernadette I will properly congratulate her. I assume Elt is the proud father?"

Jasmine shook her head yes.

"I see him all the time," related Prince. "He will receive my blessings."

"Much obliged," Jasmine said wryly. "Want to chase me?" Jasmine sprinted into the deeper grass and leaped the fence. Prince watched her dash away. He wasn't interested in the tabby's "silly games."

Meanwhile, endless thoughts raced through Jasmine's mind. Was there going to be a meeting when Elt returned? Was there going to be a celebration once the puppies arrived? Elt had no idea what was happening. He was unaware that he and Bernadette were going to be parents. So would he return from his outer space mission in time?

CHAPTER 23

"Can you please pass me the potatoes, Sweetheart?" asked Professor Greenlee. Caroline scooped a spoonful of mashed potatoes into her mouth, and then kindly obliged her father's request. "Thank you my dear," he smiled.

The Greenlees feasted on baked cinnamon chicken, mashed potatoes, corn on the cob, and buttered biscuits. Since the time machine landing and explosion in the laboratory, Stanley Greenlee had made it clear with Professor Van Hausen that he was going to spend more time with the family. A crucial part of family time for Stanley involved home-cooked meals. He adored Mrs. Greenlee's cooking, but sometimes worked too late and missed the sit-down meal time with the family.

Mrs. Greenlee was an excellent cook. Both Bryan and Caroline loved to assist their mom in the kitchen, even if the task involved only cracking eggs or cleaning spills. Family dinners always included some sort of dessert, too. Brownies and apple pie were on the sweets menu for the evening. The kids really enjoyed helping Mom with the baking of the delicacies, for "clean up" time was fun and tasty, with each child getting a chance to lick a spoonful of brownie batter.

"So, did anything exciting happen today, kids?" asked Professor Greenlee.

Bryan and Caroline smiled at each other. Bryan nodded at his sister. She laughed.

"Well," stated Bryan, "we met a new dog today. His name is Rex and he's a German Shepherd."

"Wow, where does Rex live?" inquired Mrs. Greenlee.

"Down the road," pointed Bryan. He stared at Caroline. They both began to giggle.

Professor Greenlee watched both of his kids, and then eyed Mrs. Greenlee. She shrugged and smiled. "What else happened today?"

Bryan continued to gaze at his sister. "Go ahead."

"Well, Bernadette next door…she's gonna have puppies."

Professor Greenlee finished biting into a piece of chicken. He chewed, and then wiped his mouth with a napkin. "Puppies? Isn't she kind of young to be a mommy?"

"Jenny said that she and her mom were very surprised," chimed in Bryan. "And Elt, he may be the dad."

The professor once again eyed his wife, and then engulfed a fully loaded fork full of mashed potatoes. He once again wiped his mouth. The mention of the mysterious Elt, the pooch he remembered from the time machine rescue, intrigued Stanley. "Children," he began, "I know we gabbed a little about this before, but do you recall much about the voyage on the time machine?"

"Yes Dad," the children both answered simultaneously.

Professor Greenlee paused momentarily. "Do you remember your friend Ralph…and his dog Elt…rescuing us somehow, even though they had no access to a time machine?"

"Kind of," related Caroline.

"I think it was some kind of a dream," reasoned Bryan. "For when we returned, you know after the explosion, no one was there but us. There was no Ralph, no Elt, and none of the other pets."

The professor thought quietly for a moment. The kids watched him; they could tell he was in deep thought. "I guess you're right. Some type of displacement or illusion has to be the answer to this mystery. We must have somehow managed our escape. How could Ralph, Elt, and all of those pets travel twenty-five years into the future and know exactly where we were? I guess we'll never solve that mystery."

The kids shared a meaningful look. They weren't sure what happened themselves, but they were certain that their friend, his dogs, the pets, and an alien were in the future Spring Valley. They had promised to keep a secret; whatever that secret actually was.

Professor Greenlee bit into the biscuit. Mrs. Greenlee knew that his curiosity wasn't satisfied just quite yet. "But what about the alien? How did he fit into this delusion?"

Mrs. Greenlee knew that the conversation needed to change. She cleared her throat. "Dear, did you make any new discoveries today at the observatory?"

Stanley looked up at her as though startled. He finished chewing his biscuit and then swallowed hard. "Why yes we did my dear. We observed Pluto today. I don't care what my fellow scientists say, but it will always be a planet to me."

The professor babbled for about fifteen minutes, explaining in great detail the events of the day at the lab. It was a much needed change in discussion, for the thoughts of the recent past still riddled Stanley. Why did Ralph, Elt, the neighborhood pets, and some green guy from another world all develop in their minds, including Henry Buttersample's, while twenty-five years into Spring Valley's future?

It was a mystery that the professor would never solve, but he would soon learn more secrets about the boy and the dog that lived down the street. One secret was that Elt was the possible father of Bernadette's expecting puppies. Another secret involved the extra- terrestrials that the professor knew were out there somewhere. He would soon discover more about their existence, much too close for comfort...

CHAPTER 24

"IS HE...?" VOICED SPARKY.

"I don't know," peered Elt as both canines attempted to determine whether the little Earth firefly would help return their friend and leader back to life. Myotaur was calm, but totally focused on Coladeus. Widenmauer's legs began to twitch. He awaited some sort of response from the Trianthian. Mogulus, Kraylen, and Klecktonis remained close to the regeneration chamber. The Trianthian's body was still situated in a fetal-like position.

"Should we try again?" muttered Kraylen in his alien dialect.

"Give it a little more time," eased Mogulus. "Although your Lampyridae is small, there should have been ample supply of its 'biolumens' transmitted into Coladeus's anatomy."

Mogulus examined an area on Coladeus's uniform that had been scorched. "He sustained quite a punch while under Quadrasonian control." Moments passed. There was no movement. Then all of a sudden, there was a twitch, and then another. Elt gulped, and then slowly wagged his tail. Sparky's eyes were glued on the captain.

Fingers began to flicker. The captain's head tilted slightly, and then finally, his eyes opened.

"By all the stars in the universe," heralded Kraylen in his native dialect. Mogulus smiled.

Coladeus's eyes moved about the chamber. He couldn't see anyone, but he could feel the presence of others in the room. The captain attempted to raise his head, but was still too weak. Mogulus motioned for the blue giant. Myotaur reached inside the chamber and once again retrieved his friend, placing him again on the sheet-covered lab table. Coladeus' vision began to settle in. He spotted all of his team from the last mission, plus his scientist and friend. Two unknown Trianthians walked into the lab. They rejoiced quietly when they saw what was happening.

"I trust the mission was a success?" Coladeus whispered with difficulty.

"Mission, what mission?" asked Mogulus.

Elt moved forward. He could still communicate with Mogulus. "Us…being here and the pointy heads leaving."

Mogulus nodded his head. "I'm sure the events didn't follow the plan, but all in all, it's safe to say we're safe for now."

"Excellent," sighed Coladeus. "And what about Trianthius I and II?"

Kraylen stepped closer to Coladeus. "We have sent parties to both ships, my friend. Their rescue and restoration is in progress as we speak."

"My crew and the group on Trianthius II should have been first priority," Coladeus spoke louder. "Please take care of our crews."

Kraylen signaled for Klecktonis and Myotaur. After a switch of channels on the language device, Kraylen expressed the importance of leading a couple of groups to revive and rescue the inhabitants of the impaired vessels. Once crystals were regenerated, then the two groups would embark to their respective ships.

Coladeus was able to rise and stabilize himself on the table. "Not as comfortable as I'm used to," mused the Trianthian. "But this will do."

Sparky stood and placed his two front paws on the table. He began to lick Coladeus's hand. Elt joined Sparky and greeted the captain with a tongue-full of dog kisses. The two Trianthian crewmembers walked over to Coladeus and strapped a distransulator around his neck. The captain adjusted his device.

"My friends," welcomed Coladeus.

The captain's eyes followed Mogulus as the scientist began to re-energize supplies of crystals. Mogulus stopped to present the firefly to Coladeus. "This is the reason you're here now."

Elt and Sparky watched as Coladeus closely examined the earth insect. "I've seen this species before. Who brought the specimen that saved not only my life, but Trainthius's life as well?"

"It was in old Klecky's bag," laughed Sparky.

The firefly fluttered about in its little container, its belly still glowing. Mogulus managed to provide nourishment; droplets of a dew-like substance, and a bed of leaves that resembled a miniature Earth forest for the firefly to live in. It was the scientist's utmost concern to keep that firefly alive.

The scientist delegated the crystal regeneration task to the two Trianthians that had entered the lab. The task was simple; regenerate as many crystals as possible, for they had a purpose. Elt and Sparky were about to find out their next assignment.

Mogulus adjusted his language device and approached the canines. "You two wait here. When we have accumulated the desired amount of crystals, your mission will be to help hasten Trianthius's regeneration. You will accomplish this assignment by simply dispersing crystals in strategic locations throughout our planet's exterior. The more re-energized crystals exposed to the surface, the faster Trianthius will feed itself."

"So we just fly around and dump rocks?" questioned Sparky.

"Essentially, yes," responded Mogulus with a slow smile.

"Before we feed the planet, is there any way we can feed ourselves?" asked Sparky. "I'm hungrier than a small mouth bass in a swamp filled with night crawlers."

Mogulus and Coladeus switched their attention to Elt. "Fighting that hole in the roof did drain us," affirmed Elt.

The captain and the scientist were puzzled, for they knew nothing about the dangers that the two canines had previously encountered.

"I believe all of the ingredients for your food are on board Trianthius I," related Coladeus. "We'll send for the food when we rescue the crew."

"Can you hold on a little longer?" asked Mogulus. "We are very weak; which reminds me, I need to re-energize soon."

Sparky gazed sideways at Elt. They both sighed, and then nodded. "It better be a big, granddaddy of a cheeseburger!"

Thus Elt's and Sparky's newest challenge began. After a mad dash to the regeneration chamber to boost their stone output, Elt and Sparky were issued harnesses, which contained one large pouch on either side to accommodate scores of Trianthian crystals.

"Ready to do this?" coached Sparky.

"You bet," thundered Elt. "Let's make Trianthius alive again!"

Once outside, the hungry but determined heroes spiraled their way through a maze of burnt foliage. They were outfitted with small tanks of compressed oxygen. Many of the gases that usually filled the air had dissipated due to the Quadrasonian attack rays. These gases weren't deadly to the canines; actually, they possessed elements similar to oxygen, but both Coladeus and his top scientist weren't about to take the risk.

The two finally blasted off into the Trianthian sky. The planet was naturally dark, so with the planet on very low crystal levels, the canines had difficulty navigating their way across Trianthius's terrain. Their keen eyesight aided them, but Elt and Sparky still had to be cautious, for flying too low could cause a serious accident.

Elt zoomed over a frayed stretch of forest, cupping a stone with his paw, descending and then lofting it down below. Sparky remained parallel with his partner, dropping stones in a similar fashion. Within minutes, trees began to blossom, flowers bloomed, and the grasses brightened to a fluorescent green hue. One could see where the two heroes had traveled, for flowing out behind them like the wake of a ship, was an awakened green and vibrant life, glowing like never before.

Elt and Sparky would fly for another three earth days to complete their mission. Since Trianthius was usually dark most of the time, almost dusk-like, it was difficult for Elt and Sparky to gauge how much time had actually elapsed and when it was time to stop for the day. But they figured it out.

At the end of the first day, Elt and Sparky were treated, as promised, to an incredible meal. Once the crew from Widenmauer's ship returned from Trianthius I, they delivered the food supplies designated for both humans and canines. The heroes were treated to the ultimate bacon-cheese burger, about four inches in height. Elt dove in. Although the retriever had tasted many burgers in his life, never was this combination of meat and cheese so delectable; before they knew it, the burgers were resting in their bellies.

Elt and Sparky had expended so much energy that by the time dinner was over, it was time to crash. It didn't matter where they rested. They found a small patch of shag linen that resembled a furry piece of carpet. "Sparky, do you ever think about when, you know, you were younger?" inquired Elt.

"Sure, I think about it sometimes," reminisced the retriever. "Don't remember too much though." Sparky's eyes began to close.

Elt stared at a skylight above. He stared at the endless array of stars above him, wondering which one may be home. "I think I remember my mom and dad. Do you?"

"I definitely recall my momma," Sparky said wisfully. "She was the best. I had two brothers and a sister. I don't know what happened to them. Humans came one day…young ones like ours…and boom, they were gone. One day my humans visited. Next thing I know I'm going with them. Never saw Momma again." A tear trickled down Sparky's eye. "I miss home, kid. I love being a superhero, but I also love being a dog…my human's dog."

"Me too Sparky," concluded Elt. "Me too."

Within seconds, both canines fell fast asleep. They required plenty of rest, for there was a whole planet to rejuvenate. Life on Trianthius started to glow again. The dull, lackluster yellow transformed into a vibrant, neon green. Crisp, clean rivers began to rise and flow again. Creatures that lived in the rainforest-like dwellings re-appeared from their hiding places below ground, for now the land was bountiful and healthy. Mountain ranges displayed greener textures, while the sky gleamed with a true Trianthian glow.

Matheun was the first shipmate on board Trianthius I to receive a visit to the re-generation chamber. Within minutes, though a bit unsettled, Matheun felt like his old self again, fired up and full of energy. "Where is Coladeus?" he quizzed as he stepped out of the chamber. He was assured that his captain was alive, quite well, and in good spirits.

Each Trianthian on board both vessels was treated and re-energized. Matheun was updated on the status of events, including the restoration of his species by one lone Earth insect.

"Lampyridae," stated Matheun in his alien dialogue as he shook his head in disbelief. "I would have never conceived it."

The process of restoring the two Trianthian spaceships would take a couple of Earth days, for the fuel on both crafts was totally drained. Trianthius III, which was docked at a space port and unable to respond to Trianthius I and II, towed the ships back to Trianthius, where repairs were initiated and the ships re-fueled with new, fully-charged Trianthian crystals.

Matheun was able to reunite with Coladeus as soon as he was transported down to the planet's surface. The first officer took a deep breath. "It's good to be home." Matheun pushed Coladeus' door buzzer.

"So good to see you sir," sighed Matheun once his captain opened his door. "I'm sorry I interrupted time with your family, but I wanted to make sure you were feeling better."

"I am so very humbled to see you," returned Coladeus in Trianthian speak. "The plan didn't go quite as expected, but all in all, we survived."

"Do you think the Quadrasones will return sir?" questioned Matheun.

"I do, but not here," replied Coladeus. "Somewhere else. We will reinforce our shields. Mogulus is already perfecting a defense system that will prohibit the Quadrasone's rays from penetrating our shields. It will take some time though. Widenmauer and his crew will remain here while we embark on our next mission."

Coladeus ushered Matheun towards the door.

"It was a close one sir," remarked Matheun.

"Indeed," responded Coladeus. "Rest up, regain your strength, and spend time with your family, for we will depart shortly."

"What is our next mission sir?" asked the first officer.

Coladeus stared out at the night sky as he opened the door. "We must return Elt and Sparky to their families."

CHAPTER 25

THE DAMAGED ENEMY VESSEL LIMPED through space, its engines badly burned and capability of travel doubtful. The exterior of the warship was battered and bruised, like a piece of fruit that had been left out one day too many. The ship's engines were barely operational, and life support systems were at a minimum, but there was still hope for the crew after the bitter defeat they had just faced.

The leader floated about in his chair, inspecting the repairs on the bridge. He was fidgety, for he wanted to engage the enemy, but he knew he couldn't. He was no match for the foe he had just faced. Through telepathy, he was able to communicate with all of his engineers; to assess the carnage to his warship, his pride and joy.

Where had he gone wrong? Victory had been in his grasp, yet it was taken away by some unseen force; a ship that was bigger and stronger. How did this foe launch a sneak attack? And the most important mystery was "What happened to Coladeus?"

Zemak fumed about the ship. Not one of his crew wished to confront him with any updates on the status of his ship, since the news wasn't good. So it was better just to message him and face his wrath later.

Zemak and his first officer toured the engine facility area. Smoke from the recent fires permeated the room. Huge beams dangled from the ceilings high above. Crews were already working on re-securing the beams, but it would take time.

"We are at about fifty percent of capability," transmitted Dresant through mind-speak in his native language. "Our shields and accelerators should be fully operational soon. Life support systems are improving."

Zemak continued to inspect the area. "And our weaponry?"

"Our ray transmittal device sustained heavy damages. We will have to wait until the ship regains full power before we can seriously reinstate our weapons program."

"Any crew casualties?" asked the leader.

"No, but we did sustain some injuries."

Zemak began to stare ahead. Dresant wasn't quite sure what his leader was staring at. Zemak loathed defeat. Coladeus, whether he was dead or alive, wasn't going to get the best of him. He knew the Trianthians were defeated. There was no way Trianthius would have survived the barrage of attacks they had presented. The planet's restoration, if possible, would take duraceps to complete. Zemak knew nothing about the firefly.

After a briefing concerning the rest of the ship, and a quick visit to the injured, Zemak headed back to the bridge.

"Sir, when we do embark, have you made plans for our next voyage?" inquired the first officer.

"I have." Zemak stopped and turned toward Dresant. "It is imperative that we locate Coladeus. If for some reason he is still alive, we will capture Coladeus and end his life once and for all!"

CHAPTER 26

"SO WHAT DO YOU THINK?" asked Jenny.

Ralph heard Jenny's question, but wasn't totally focused. A week and a half had passed and yet his Elt hadn't returned from the mission to presumably save Coladeus and the Trianthians. What had happened? Did anything go astray on the mission?

Ralph had cried a couple of times late at night, but he knew that he had to keep it together, for he too was part of the mission. Ralph had to have faith that his dog would return. He prayed for Elt's safe arrival daily.

"I mean is that, like okay with you?" asked Jenny. "You know, to have the party together? Before Bernie has her puppies?"

Ralph was both overwhelmed and distracted. He gazed down at his feet as he walked. As they all walked to school together, his friends were conversing about a birthday party. All Ralph could think about was his dog coming home.

"I think it's a grand idea," chimed in Caroline. "A birthday party for Elt and Bernadette. It will be fun!" Now Ralph had figured that

Elt's official birthday had already passed, or was close to passing, for his pooch was about six weeks old when he received Elt for his own birthday. So the boy treated his own birthday and Elt's as the same day. It was easier for him to remember.

It was mid-September. In less than a month, Ralph would turn eleven, and he and his dog would celebrate their birthdays. Better yet, his best friend's dog would be bearing pups soon. It was hard to believe that one short year ago, both Elt and Bernadette were puppies themselves. Now fully grown, they were ready to start a family of their own. Life was changing, for both canines and humans in the Valleydale subdivision.

Ralph attempted to keep himself occupied during Elt's absence. Primarily, he carried on with his regular routine: school, chores, and walks with his friends and Oleo. The group continued to trek their normal route, but finished up on Spring Drive, and a visit with Rex. Sometimes the German Shepherd would be there to greet them; other times he would stay inside. Ralph and his friends were still pretty hesitant about petting him, for they weren't quite sure how friendly he would be without Zach there beside the shepherd. Rex was intimidating, much like Prince the Doberman.

Ralph worked on his project for a couple of days. He knew that the project idea that he had formulated to cover the need for the piece of sheet metal couldn't disappear, for Mr. Eltison was truly excited about viewing the final outcome. After hours of indecisiveness, Ralph, with Oleo by his side, brainstormed like he had never done before. Ralph could work under pressure, and make quick decisions. He had pushed Elt's stone when it was time to rescue the time travelers. But creating something out of a bunch of stray building materials; that wasn't Ralph at all.

Ralph's dad was amazed that his son had spent so much time working on the project, and had not given up on the idea. He sensed that his boy was maturing and taking responsibility. When it was time for the unveiling, Ralph invited his dad down to the shed. Dad had been kindly forbidden to enter until the creation had been completed.

"Wow!" was Mr. Eltison's reaction. He examined the detail in Ralph's handcraft. "Interesting. Where did you come up with the idea?"

Ralph knew that his dad was being polite, but what he didn't realize was that for an almost-eleven year-old, his creation was very good. "Well, I kind of messed up on that big piece," fibbed Ralph, knowing that the piece he purchased at Feldman's was used to repair the alien spacecraft. "So I kind of found some pieces lying around, and I discovered the wheels in that can over there. I hope that was okay."

"Does it go in the water too?" asked Mr. Eltison.

"Yes Sir," responded Ralph. "I don't know what to call it, but it can drive into the water, float like a boat, and see these wings?" It can fly too."

Ralph's dad shook his head. "Ralph, I don't know what to say, well I do know what to say...just one more word...Ingenious!"

"Really?" asked Ralph. The boy felt somewhat positive about his project, but didn't expect his dad to favor it.

"Did you realize that the military has a line of vehicles that can navigate on both land and water?" inquired Ralph's dad. "And that there are seaplanes that land on water?"

"I was aware of the seaplanes," Ralph answered. "I didn't know about the ones that go on land and in the water."

"I think the army calls them amphibious rovers or something like that," mentioned Ralph's dad. "But you've created a model that can ride, float, and fly. Simply amazing!"

Ralph smiled. He could see that his dad was proud. He liked making his Dad proud.

"Are you going to bring it inside tonight?"

Ralph thought for a few seconds. "Maybe I'll take it to my room."

"Sounds like a plan." Ralph's dad began to walk away from the shed.

"Dad?"

"Yes son?"

"Jenny would like to host a birthday party for both Elt and Bernadette at her house. Do dogs get birthday parties?"

"Why not?" smiled Mr. Eltison. "Are parents invited?"

"Sure, I guess," answered Ralph. He closed the shed door. He would return later to retrieve his model. "She hasn't picked the date yet, but it will probably co...what's the word...co...coinci...?"

"Coincide?" Ralph's dad offered.

"Right…coincide with the time Bernadette and Elt came to live with Jenny and me."

Ralph was pleased with Jenny's idea, but hoped it would be later than sooner. Although Oleo had perfected his replication role of Elt, he didn't want the Sorgian at Jenny's home for the birthday party. Oleo followed Ralph and Mr. Eltison inside the house.

"Oh, by the way," mentioned Mr. Eltison. "Since we're talking about Elt's birthday, the vet's office called today."

All of the elation from the last few minutes stopped instantly, for Ralph sensed the unexpected curve ball that his dad was about to throw him.

"Yeah, I scheduled Elt's one year appointment for later this week," continued Mr. Eltison. "I'll have to check the date and time again, but I believe it's this Friday after you come home from school."

A lump formed in Ralph's throat. "What type of appointment?"

"You know, a one year check-up," assured Mr. Eltison. "Elt may require a shot or two. Dr. Kelly will check his heart, his breathing, things like that. Maybe it's time to talk to her about Elt…you know… getting 'fixed'."

Ralph was still stuck on the first line -- a vet's appointment on Friday. What if Oleo was still there? What in the world would happen when Dr. Kelly examined the replicate? What would she discover?

There had been only one occasion when Oleo had temporarily "lost" Elt's identity, like the night he "showed" his true self to Jasmine and Bernadette during Elt's mission to Titan. Ralph noticed it one night before he fell asleep. Luckily, there was never another occurrence in front of his friends or Mr. Eltison. But what if it happened in Dr. Kelly's office? A million thoughts raced through Ralph's brain. Then his dad's later comment hit him.

"Fixed? Wait, did Elt break something?"

Mr. Eltison smiled. "Oh no, with all the talk about Bernadette having only one litter of puppies, it might be a good idea that we talk to Dr. Kelly about…" Ralph shook his head. He now understood, but Elt wasn't Elt right now. What if Dr. Kelly discovered some type of alien life form inhabiting Elt's body and brain? What if Oleo didn't have the same heartbeat as Elt? What if he didn't have a heart at all? This certainly was not good.

Before Ralph retired for the evening, he hoped and prayed for Elt's safe return. He racked his brain to come up with some sort of a plan. He could fake a sickness, but that was too risky, for Ralph knew his dad. The boy would be left at home to rest in his room while his dad took Elt to the vet's office. Ralph couldn't think of anything.

When Friday did arrive, his dad was waiting for him to come home from school. "Ralph, you ready to go? Find Elt's leash."

There was no time to react. "I just got home. Do I have time for a snack?"

"A quick one, and then we have to go," directed Mr. Eltison from his office.

Ralph grabbed a cookie from a cookie jar on the counter. Munching it, he walked into his room. Since Oleo's second time there at his house, it had been customary for the replicate to welcome Ralph home with his tail wagging and a couple of puppy kisses. This day was different though, for when Ralph walked into his room, his canine was asleep on his bed.

"Wow, you don't know what you're in for today Oleo," Ralph stated.

The pooch rose slowly and stretched. He walked over to Ralph and started kissing him, but not too excitedly. "Come on boy," Ralph gestured. The canine slowly followed his human. Ralph attached the leash onto the hook of his neon green collar. Within minutes, Mr. Eltison, Ralph, and the canine boarded the pick-up truck and soon arrived at Dr. Kelly's office.

"You must know something is up," thought Ralph to himself, for Oleo seemed solemn and non-responsive as they sat in the waiting room. Maybe that was the way Sorgians acted when they were timid or scared. Soon Ralph, his dad, and the canine were ushered into one of the examination rooms. The dog was weighed. Sixty-eight pounds. So far so good. Dr. Kelly entered the room. After a brief greeting, she reached for her stethoscope. It was the moment of truth.

"Heart sounds good," she said matter of factly.

Ralph was stunned. Did Sorgians change their entire identity, including their organs? That just wasn't possible. Ralph blinked.

Nonchalantly, he began to pat his dog on the head. Then he reached for his collar and felt its underside, and there it was. The stone! What???

Ralph bent down to examine his dog, trying not to impede on Dr. Kelly's examination. Elt began to wag his tail. Ralph was speechless. How did Elt fool him? His dog was home. He never had the chance to say good-bye to Oleo, but it didn't matter. His dog was with him.

"Everything okay, Bud?" asked Mr. Eltison.

Ralph smiled. "Yes Dad, everything's ok."

What no one had seen before Ralph returned home from school that afternoon, and while Mr. Eltison was working in his office, was when Oleo wandered outside through the doggie door. One second the replicate was walking past Elt's doghouse, the next, he appeared on Trianthius I. Seconds later, Elt appeared from behind his doghouse. The super dog, who had exerted copious amounts of energy during the mission, was still quite fatigued from the work and the trip.

Elt had taken care of business, walked into the kitchen, nibbled on some dry dogfood, and then jumped onto Ralph's bed. By the position of the sun in the sky, Elt had determined that Ralph would be home soon. He had curled up in a ball and fallen asleep. He was awakened by his human, hours later just before the trip to the vet's office.

"Well, I'm impressed with the excellent job you're doing with Elt," summarized Dr. Kelly.

Ralph took a deep breath and sighed. "I figured everything was good. I don't know why I was so scared."

"That's quite normal," declared Dr. Kelly. "A trip to my office sometimes means kind of scary things, but this was a wellness check, just to make sure Elt was staying healthy. How is he running and playing? I'm sure he's pretty strong."

"You can say that," grinned Ralph. She had no idea.

Elt received immunizations for heartworm, distemper, and rabies that day; all very threatening sicknesses that needed prevention with inoculations. Ralph hugged his dog. Then they headed to the car together.

"I think it's time to celebrate," rejoiced Mr. Eltison. "It's Friday. Let's drop Elt off and head over to Brown's. I haven't had one of their steaks in ages."

"Sounds good, Dad," added Ralph. "But after dinner, I want to spend extra time with Elt. "I feel like I haven't seen him in weeks."

"Consider it done," smiled Ralph's dad.

At dinner, Ralph scoffed down a Brown's famous burger; his dad dined on a steak, medium rare, baked potato, and a salad. Ralph wanted to share the great news of Elt's return, but he knew he couldn't. Keeping secrets about his dog was difficult; how he wanted to share the stories with someone! After finishing their scrumptious dinner, they headed back home, but before the day turned to dusk, Ralph and Elt played catch with a stick in the yard. On a couple of occasions, with his dad inside and hopefully not peering through the kitchen window, the boy tossed the stick high up in the air. Elt still possessed his incredible leaping ability. Ralph was truly blessed. His dog was back, safe and sound. Whatever the mission was, it hopefully was a successful one. How Ralph wished he could speak with Elt.

Ralph didn't want to fall asleep that night. He and his dog played outside well into the darkness of night. There was no school the next day, so there was no objection from Mr. Eltison. He was proud of his son. The project...there were no issues at school so far...and he had handled every imaginable responsibility when it came to taking care of his pet, just like he said he would one year ago.

Ralph showered just before bed. Elt followed his human into the kitchen, where the boy shared the few remaining doggie treats that Oleo didn't devour. "I don't ever want you to go on a mission in space again," whispered Ralph as he snuggled with his pet. "I really thought I lost you this time."

Elt too, thought about his latest trip to Trianthius. He had missed home, Ralph, Bernadette and all of his friends. He and Sparky had almost lost their lives in Klecktonis's ship. However, he had just aided an entire species, preventing their complete demise. Better yet, his friend and leader, Coladeus, was alive. Wasn't that what all this superhero business was all about?

"Is Coladeus okay boy?" Ralph's eyes were about to close. Within minutes, the boy was in a deep slumber. Elt too was exhausted but he had to stay awake, for he had to visit Bernadette.

The super dog crept out quietly, for he didn't want to stir Ralph or his dad. Everything was so strange to Elt, even though this was his home. He could smell Oleo's scent throughout the house and yard. Elt poked his head through Bernadette's doggie door. He had to be careful. Just because all of the lights were out didn't mean that all the humans were asleep. Also, he didn't want to startle Bernadette. In the darkness of the Rodgers' kitchen, Elt stretched one foreleg through the doggie door and tapped the floor softly with his paw. Bernadette heard the noise. She started to growl, but something inside prevented the spaniel from barking. She ran into the kitchen and the two dogs wiggled through the doggie door outside.

Bernadette brushed up against Elt. How she had missed him, but now her mate was home! After a briefing about the mission from Elt, it was time for Bernadette to relate the news. Elt was about to encounter a new mission – fatherhood.

CHAPTER 27

BESIDES RESTORING MAGNUS I BACK into operation, Professor Greenlee was able to convince Professor Van Hausen to update some satellite software on their computers, enabling their researchers to view pictures of space during the day. It was shortly before noon when student Amanda Walker was working in the observatory and casually watching the feed from outer space. Suddenly, an alert sounded on her computer. She moved toward the monitor. Amanda couldn't believe her eyes! There was something just outside of Earth's atmosphere. Was it another satellite, a probe, or a UFO? She quickly clicked on the print icon. When she examined the screen again, it was gone.

"Uh, Professor?" called Amanda. Greenlee had stepped out to grab a cup of coffee. Sweat began to pour down Amanda's face as the image printed out in front of her. She definitely discovered something, but what was it? It resembled a dark spot on the photo.

When Professor Greenlee returned, Amanda presented him with the photo, and then showed him the image on screen. He set down his cup and scanned the evidence before him. "What did you see Amanda?"

"It's hard to say Professor," Amanda replied. "It was there, as you can see on the picture. When I looked again, it disappeared."

"Whatever it was, it's gone now," commented a disappointed Professor Greenlee. "What an unfortunate time to grab a cup of joe."

The two attempted to enhance and enlarge the photo, but it was still too sketchy to ascertain. Their UFO had vanished, but at least they had some sort of proof. Later that evening, the professor and his assistant stayed late in order to view Magnus I. It was a starry night, and the view was incredible, but there was no sign of their discovery.

Trianthius I was gone, but it would appear again soon. So would a not-so-friendly ship, one set on destruction and the demise of a Trianthian leader named Coladeus.

CHAPTER 28

THE WARSHIP SOARED METHODICALLY THROUGH deep space. In about an equivalent to a month of earth time, most of the ship's repairs had been completed. Its only setback was its defense shields, which had been severely damaged by the arachnid's arsenal. That process would take time and a port to house the ship for a proper repair. Another factor was that the Quadrasonian leader was too impatient to wait for the repair time. Zemak had one plan. Success had eluded him. He would forge onward until Coladeus was both defeated and demised.

"Do they know we are following them?" transmitted Zemak in his native thought-speak.

"No sir," assured Dresant. "We are keeping a safe distance so they will not track us."

The leader stared straight ahead at the holographic image of deep space before him. "Somehow they have managed to regain their power. They had no power. Coladeus was dead. How did they survive?"

"It appears they found a way, Sir," replied Dresant. "We are formulating a theory on their incredible rejuvenation."

Zemak continued to stare at the image. There was nothing but darkness and the twinkling of distant planets and stars. "The destroyers that surprised us...do we have any confirmation of their presence in the area?" The leader referred to the surprise rescue attack from the arachnids.

"Negative," replied the first officer. "We had no record of their existence. We're not sure of their affiliation with the Trianthians. They did surprise us, Sir."

"Do we have any knowledge of the Trianthian's destination?" returned Zemak.

Dresant scanned his screen for the desired information. "The Trianthian vessel stopped briefly at the third planet in this system that revolves around its sun."

"We've traveled to that planet before, haven't we?" asked the leader.

"Affirmative," replied Dresant. "Should we set our course sir?"

"Yes, yes," gleamed Zemak. "When the time is right, we will invade this planet; use our intrusion as a trap. I suspect that Coladeus is still alive and onboard that ship. We will destroy Coladeus and his crew once and for all."

Zemak sat back on his chair and floated out of the bridge area.

* * *

Trianthius I resumed its normal speed somewhere between Earth and Venus. Their immediate mission, a simple one, was to simply check on the status of Venus, Klecktonis's home planet. Coladeus had assured the space hero that Trianthius I would pay a visit during her brief stay on Trianthius with Widenmauer and Myotaur. Even though she was pretty certain that the Quadrasones had no knowledge of her and the connection she had with Coladeus, Klecktonis was still worried about any retaliation set forth by the aggressive pointy-heads.

A couple of earth weeks had lapsed since the pivotal battle just outside of Trianthius was won by the arachnids. The Trianthian race had been saved; both the planet and the citizens had been reborn with the glow from one firefly. Trianthius had returned to its original state.

Once the planet was revitalized, it was time for the crew of the Trianthian vessels to begin repairs to the ship and yes, prepare for their next voyages. Not even a close call of extinction ever phased Coladeus. He knew that their missions must continue.

Trianthius I and II were both re-energized, the engines tested for battle. Most importantly, a new wrinkle in the defense system was installed. Mogulus was quite confident that the updates to the defense shields were impenetrable by the Quadrasonian ray. Through a thorough and disciplined search, Mogulus discovered the source of the deadly ray and its origin. He discovered a formula that would counteract that element.

Once the spaceships passed all of their qualifying examinations and simulations, the ships were cleared for take-off. After a day of rest from their project of restoring the planet, Elt and Sparky were blasted off into space, en route to Earth. Elt and Sparky were reunited with their humans and the replicates returned to Trianthius I. Coladeus set the ship's course for Venus. It wasn't long before Trianthius I would encounter their next duel with the Quadrasones.

"Do you still have confirmation that we are being followed?" questioned Coladeus to his first officer in his Trianthian dialect.

"That is affirmative," confirmed Matheun. "According to my readings, their warship is closing in on Earth."

"And the Quadrasones are unaware that we have detected their presence?" returned the captain.

"Yes sir," replied Matheun. "New updates to our intelligence software have greatly enhanced our spying abilities. Mogulus has succeeded."

A crewmember handed the captain a tablet. He scanned the message and then returned it back to the shipmate. "And our special project is ready for the pilot just in case a situation arises?" questioned Coladeus.

"Yes sir. I'm sure the Quadrasones will be surprised."

"Do we still have contact with our former agents on Earth?" was Coladeus's last inquiry.

"I believe they can still be reached sir," answered the first officer. "I'm not sure about the status of their crystals."

"Excellent! Prepare a stone for each of them just in case," instructed the leader.

Matheun turned around to face his captain. "Sir, do you feel Zemak knows you're alive?"

Coladeus smiled momentarily. "I'm sure his instincts have led them to us, but we'll be ready for his next move." Trianthius I stayed on course for Venus. It was only a matter of time before Coladeus would once again be confronted with the enemy. This time they would be prepared, but the only question was, "What was Zemak's next move?"

CHAPTER 29

"CAN YOU HAND ME THE streamers on the table please?" asked Jenny. Ralph obliged. With his assistance, she scaled the step ladder and hung various colored streamers throughout the living and dining room areas.

Almost a month had passed, and all was serene in Spring Valley. Life had gleefully returned to normalcy for Ralph and Elt; life fell into the rhythm of school, chores, time with friends and their pets during their walks, along with private time with his pooch. Ralph was elated to have his dog back. The stone attached to Elt's collar had been silent, and there were no other signs of direct contact with Coladeus or any other space alien. Ralph wondered about the fortunes of the Trianthians. He also thought about Sparky. How he wished he could dog-speak with his pet, so he could be assured that the Trianthian leader and Golden Retriever super dog were in good health. Hopefully the downtime would continue, but for now, life was good. There were celebrations for birthdays and puppies to plan.

Elt and Bernadette didn't quite know how to react to all of the excitement that was occurring at the Rodgers' house. Neither pet really understood what a birthday party was about, but soon they were going to discover that this event in their honor was something both special and fun. Although the party was the main reason for the celebration, the arrival of the puppies was on every human's mind.

Jenny showed Ralph an area just inside the laundry room, which was offset from the kitchen, where she and her mom had created a "puppy place" for Bernadette and her new arrivals. A crate was lined with comfy blankets and old sheets. Jenny found an unused lamp in the attic. It provided just enough soft light for Bernadette and her young.

Bryan and Caroline were invited to attend the party, along with a couple of friends from school. The Greenlee children attempted to escort Trixie over for the party, but the poodle became apprehensive when it was time to enter the Rodger's house. Trixie sensed there was something going on that involved Elt and Bernadette, and wanted no part of it. There was still a touch of jealousy in the poodle, for she remembered the day that Elt was mesmerized by her own presence.

Ms. Rodgers prepared burgers, hot dogs, and tacos for the human main course. Then there were the desserts: apple pie with ice cream, pudding, and brownies. Ralph's dad would stop by later when the festivities began, but Ralph and Elt were there at Jenny's house early to help Ms. Rodgers prepare.

Bernadette waddled from place to place in the living and dining rooms. Elt waited for her to find a comfy spot and sat down beside her. Jenny and her mom knew that it would be any day now. There was no telling how just how many puppies there would be.

"Are you going to keep all the puppies?" Caroline had asked in a prior conversation.

"We're not sure right now," answered Jenny. "We'll have to see how many there are. We'll probably find homes for most of them."

There were plenty of treats for the birthday pooches, too. A mixed bowl of doggie delicacies, including small chew-bones, miniature steak morsels, and wrapped chicken yummies lined a bowl that was next to the presents for Elt and Bernadette. Although she was pleased with her surroundings, Bernadette could barely touch her food, for there wasn't much room in her tummy. Ralph threw a bunch of treats in a plastic bag, for the neighborhood dogs would receive a "surprise" the next day when he passed them by.

Elt easily scarfed his portion of the birthday bonanza. The celebration reminded him of special occasions like wet dogfood days and Thanksgiving dinner. Once he sniffed the tantalizing aroma of Ralph's cheeseburger, he recalled the time not too long ago of the Trianthian creation that he and Sparky dined on. Ralph was surprised to see his dog staring at him with loving eyes. Ralph couldn't resist, and shared his burger with his pooch.

Jenny and her mom organized a few games that the kids could play with the pets. A fetch game was easy for Elt. Bernadette participated for a short time, but then retired to a spot on the carpet beside the couch to rest. Mr. Eltison helped Ms. Rodgers with the dishes while the kids found some board games to play in the living room. By nine o'clock, it was time for the party to "wrap up."

"Keep us posted if the puppies arrive," urged Caroline as she headed out.

"We're gonna ask me mum and dad if we can have one of them," added Bryan.

Jenny grinned and waved bye. Ralph helped his friend straighten the living room. "Mom says we can keep the streamers up for a day or two. By the way, it's your birthday soon, right?" Ralph nodded. "Are you thinking of having a party?" asked Jenny.

Ralph thought for a second or two. "Not sure yet. I've been kind of thinking about Bernadette and her pups. Do you really think Elt is the dad?"

"I guess we'll find out soon," grinned Jenny. "If any of them that resemble Elt show up, then we'll know."

The two friends walked outside. Elt and Bernadette followed. The boy and his friend sat down on the side porch. It was a pleasant fall evening, not a cloud in the sky. The air was cool, but not quite enough for a sweater or jacket. The kids stared up at the starry field above them. They were met by Jasmine the tabby, who had watched the nightly events earlier through an outside window ledge. Jasmine rubbed her head up against Jenny's leg.

"You ever think about you mom when you're gazing at the stars?" Jenny asked quietly. Jenny had never mentioned Ralph's mom before.

"Sometimes," answered Ralph. He wasn't upset, for he knew that Jenny's question was genuine.

"I think of my dad sometimes when I look up at stars," related Jenny.

Ralph paused momentarily as they both continued to scan the sky. Jenny had never mentioned a word about her father before. Ralph had wondered, but had never gathered the courage to ask Jenny.

"How did…?" asked Ralph.

"I'll tell you one day," interrupted Jenny. "I just really love watching the stars. I can't wait to study them one day at the observatory. Who knows what I might see."

Oh how Ralph wanted to share the stories of outer space he had recently encountered with his friend. "It must be really something up there, huh?" Jenny smiled.

The door opened then and Mr. Eltison stepped out. "Time to head home, Bud."

Ralph stood and turned around. "See ya tomorrow. Call me, you know, if the puppies…."

"Will do," said Jenny. "I'm a little nervous for her right now."

"Bernadette is going to be fine," assured Ralph's dad.

"Yeah, she's gonna be an awesome mom," confirmed Ralph.

Ralph, his dad, and Elt all ventured home. Within an hour, all three were in bed. Little did they know that their evening was just about to begin.

CHAPTER 30

I̲t̲ ̲w̲a̲s̲ ̲a̲ ̲l̲a̲t̲e̲ ̲n̲i̲g̲h̲t̲ for Professor Greenlee. The clear starry night provided a perfect backdrop for a night of exploration for him and his students. Even Professor Van Hausen had stopped by earlier to "take a gander" at some of the truly breathtaking views through the lenses of Magnus I. Amanda and a number of her fellow student associates had left already, for it was close to midnight. The professor knew that he was working way beyond his normal shift, but ever since the day Amanda had discovered the strange spot on the surveillance photos, Greenlee was determined to discover its identity and spot it again with the assistance of his amazing telescope.

Before closing up for the evening, the professor decided to take one last look. It was a wise move on his part. At first, the professor couldn't believe his eyes. Surely his eyes were playing tricks on him. Sweat began to bead on his brow as he focused in on the subject. At first, there was just one object. Suddenly, one sprung from the original, then another, and another. Was it some kind of test flight the air force was conducting? This late at night? Hardly. Besides, to the best of Stanley's knowledge, the air force hadn't created anything that resembled what he was presently witnessing.

The objects began to draw closer. Greenlee stumbled back for a moment, and then attempted to collect himself. What was the protocol for this type of event? He had to inform someone! Maybe someone already knew. He took one last look. The smaller shadows darted off in different directions. Were they ships? If so, they seemed to be heading straight for him. Could Earth be under attack? What Professor Greenlee didn't know was that the smaller vessels were entering the planet's atmosphere on their way to two destinations: San Francisco and Spring Valley!

CHAPTER 31

ELT SENSED SOMETHING WRONG. HE didn't bark or growl, for he didn't want to arouse Ralph or Mr. Eltison. He jumped out of bed, paced around the living room for a short time, and then decided to dart out the doggie door. It was a calm night, a perfect continuation of a splendid evening just a few hours before. Elt sniffed the outside air. "Seems quiet, but something's not right."

"Hey, how was the party?" asked a familiar voice. Jasmine appeared out from the shadows of the night.

Elt wasn't attempting to be rude or evasive, but he ignored her comment. Something bad was about to happen. "Sorry Jasmine. Listen. Do you hear anything?"

Jasmine sniffed and scanned the area around Springhaven Court. "Crickets…bugs?"

Elt shook his head. "No, something else. Something's wrong."

Cats possessed a keen sense for danger, but for some reason that evening, Jasmine wasn't feeling it. Elt heard Chin barking in the yard across the way. The Chow-Chow was always aware of his surroundings.

Chin's messages were the same as the way Elt felt. Something was wrong, but Chin couldn't put his paw on it either.

"I'll be back," gestured Elt. "Go warn the others."

"Warn 'em about what?" purred a puzzled Jasmine.

"Something is here…not from this world…a presence. I don't know. Please just warn them…especially Bernadette."

Elt dashed back to check in on his humans. Jasmine began to shrug off her friend's request, and that's when it happened. From a distance, the first "boom" occurred. An explosion of that magnitude was matched only once in Spring Valley; the night the time machine was destroyed. This was no time machine.

Ralph and his dad heard the disturbance. Elt ran into the boy's room. Ralph jumped out of bed immediately. "What is it boy?" Elt barked a couple of times. He gazed right into his human's eyes. Ralph realized that there was some kind of trouble brewing and that it was Elt's duty to investigate and hopefully save his town.

Elt began to take off. "Wait boy!" He hugged his dog. Ralph had to act quickly. He twisted Elt's collar and pushed the button on the stone. The stone brightened, just like it had before the time traveler's mission. Ralph was convinced that whatever was out there, Elt couldn't handle it alone. "Go boy!"

Mr. Eltison trounced into his son's bedroom. "You okay Ralph?"

"Yeah Dad."

"Stay in here until I check everything out."

Elt's first instinct was to check on Bernadette. As he closed in on Jenny's house, Professor Greenlee's car crashed through the gate that led to the Greenlee driveway. Frantic, the professor leaped out of his vehicle yelling "The aliens are here! They're here! It's the end of the world! Darling! Kids! Wake up!"

Aliens! He knew it. Elt flashed up onto Bernadette's back porch. There was another massive explosion in the distance. Elt heard Sarge join Chin in the urgent serenade of howls and barks. Elt carefully stuck his head inside the doggie door. Oddly, there were many lights on inside. He could hear Bernadette whimpering, but he couldn't see her. Ms. Rodgers moved about, running from room to room in a hectic pace. Jenny raced into the kitchen and opened some drawers. "These towels Mom?"

"No, the old ones in the hall closet," returned Jenny's mom from another room.

Elt was confused. He wanted to make sure Bernadette was okay, but he didn't want to be seen by her humans. He didn't realize that it was that time…Bernadette was about to give birth to her first puppy. He turned and headed in the direction of the explosions.

Jasmine haphazardly sped from one yard to another, now coming to grips with Elt's intuitions…something wasn't right, and it wasn't from this world. She targeted Sarge first. The Boxer, definitely troubled by the presence of some unknown entity, paced throughout his yard.

"My human is upset!" charged Sarge. "I'm a little frightened myself. What's going on?"

"Elt is going to check it out," assured Jasmine. She whisked away in the direction of Trixie and Seymour. Once she witnessed Professor Greenlee slamming his car into the yard, Jasmine re-directed her course, and headed to Chin's. The Chow-Chow continued his barking, so she figured he was "on his game" and ready to protect his home from any precarious encounter.

The tabby gasped for air and attempted to collect her thoughts. She stepped toward Prince's house and then stopped. "Bernadette!" Jasmine raced over to her friend's house and thumped through the doggie door. She wasn't worried about being seen. Something was up though. She had never entered another human's house, but her instincts told her that something was going on with the mother-to-be. Then she noticed the three of them, Jenny and her mom, pacing and worrying, and Bernadette lying in her little bed in the laundry room. Everything was calm.

Jenny spotted Jasmine first. "Come here girl," Jenny pleaded. Jasmine shyly walked over to the girl and sat down between Jenny and her mom. "Look Mom, she knows."

Ms. Rodgers smiled. "Ya think so, huh?"

"Stay here and help us," trusted Jenny.

Whatever was going on outside didn't matter. In the Rodgers's house, there was plenty of drama going on. Jasmine knew where she belonged during the crisis. She stayed with Bernadette.

Elt thought about running all the way to where the explosions were occurring, but he thought otherwise. Who was going to see what he was about to do in the middle of the night with all of the chaos happening? Elt blasted off into the night sky.

It was merely seconds before Elt reached his destination; downtown Spring Valley. Although there were no citizens walking the streets in the middle of the night, there were residents who were running for their lives. Elt halted and hovered in mid-flight. There was no Sparky…no Trinathians…just him. What was he going to do?

There were three mini-sized space fighters, the same ones Coladeus and the space heroes had witnessed on Titan, firing stinging rays at structures and parked cars. Fires erupted on the street and in some buildings. White's Drug Store and the Towne Bakery Shoppe sustained some damages; the Spring Valley Public Library's entrance was severely struck.

Deputy Taylor was on call that evening. Since the time Crum and his men were detained and cast out of Spring Valley, Sheriff Thomas and Deputy Taylor worked mostly day hours, but were "on call" for certain nights if situations arose. This catastrophe was definitely a time when the deputy received an urgent message from the 911 emergency operator.

"Aliens in spaceships attacking Spring Valley?" gawked Deputy Taylor. He had heard the explosions moments earlier, but would have never attributed the disturbance to an alien invasion. There had to be a better explanation. The deputy called his boss for assistance. Should they call the Army? The National Guard? The situation had to be investigated first before calls could be made.

Elt knew he had to act fast, for the pointy-heads, the Quadrasones, were attempting to devastate as much of the town as they could. The ships drew closer to the super dog. He only had seconds to formulate a plan.

CHAPTER 32

SPARKY HEARD THE TRANSMISSION EMANATING from his stone. It was a warning from Coladeus. Danger was imminent. San Francisco was about to be infiltrated by the Quadrasones, but Sparky didn't have all the facts. There was one main concern; San Francisco was in a later time zone, so it wasn't after midnight in the big city. Many folks weren't asleep yet. A certain twelve year-old was just going to bed.

Amy Pendergrass had noticed the change in her canine once again. For the last few weeks, her dog was "Sparky" again; running, fetching, swimming, and most imperatively, surfing. The differences in eating were minimal, for the Sorgian, Rat, had loved cheeseburgers and even regular dog food. Nevertheless, Amy continued to monitor her dog because of the disparities, which made the twelve year-old suspicious. Why did her dog act so differently sometimes?

Sparky attempted to silence the garbled message emanating from his stone by maneuvering his head closer to his neck. Amy wouldn't have understood the dog-speak dialect, but the sudden noise might have awakened her. Sparky quietly skitted out of Amy's bedroom.

Amy had never fallen into a deep sleep, so all of Sparky's movement on her bed awakened her. Curious, Amy crept out of bed and followed her dog. She tip-toed down the stairs and eased into the kitchen. Amy couldn't see Sparky at all, for the light in the kitchen was faint. The girl didn't want to alert her parents by turning on a light. She wasn't sure if one of them was still awake.

Amy poked her head through the doggie door. The moon's glimmer of light provided Amy a shadowed glimpse of her Sparky, standing in the outer edge of the backyard. She quietly opened the door, slithered through the opening, and attempted to trace her dog's steps. In the distance, Amy could hear a scratchy sound, like the music her dad played in the back office at the Coconut Waves, but she wasn't quite sure what it was. Where was Sparky going? What was that noise?

As she scrambled down the stairs, Amy lost sight of Sparky. Then in a flash, Amy witnessed an unbelievable sight. Her Sparky was up in the air…flying. "I must still be asleep. This must be a dream," she thought. Amy rubbed her eyes, but Sparky was still there, and then he flew off towards the inner city.

"Sparky?" whispered Amy. "What's going on?"

The simple message that had been transmitted via Sparky's stone was that the Quadrasones had deployed a small squadron of fighters into the city; their motive was unknown. It was possible that the deployment was a diversion; a plan elsewhere may be set to either take over Earth or draw Coladeus closer to the planet. Sparky's mission: attempt to thwart the plan by defeating the enemy fighters.

Why did the Quadrasones choose San Francisco and Spring Valley and not bigger cities like New York City or Washington, D.C? Simple. The Quadrasones were an aggressive species, but their numbers were minimal. Their only arsenal was the warship, and it only possessed the five fighter ships. Secondly, the warship tapped into where the Trianthians had made their last transmissions…San Francisco and Spring Valley (where Sparky and Elt had departed from). The Quadrsones wanted to set a trap to create chaos in order to draw Coladeus to Earth, if indeed, the Trianthian was still alive.

The night air breezed against Sparky's whiskers as he scanned the city below him. He spotted the first sign of trouble. A Quadrasonian space fighter, like the one he witnessed on Titan, was firing laser shots at the Golden Gate Bridge. Like Elt, Sparky had to formulate a plan that involved one outcome...don't get obliterated by any of the enemy's laser beams!

The retriever closed in on the fighter. He held no weapons; he only possessed his speed and agility, along with his ability to fly. Surfing wasn't going to help his cause, but he did think of an awesome idea that involved the bay and one of his old adversaries. As the pointy-headed pilot closed in on a section of the bridge, Sparky whizzed by like a pesky gnat on a hot summer day. The retriever tapped on the window glass with his paw and smiled. "Hey pointy-heads, why don't you try to catch old Sparky."

The Golden Retriever stayed close to the ship, out of the direct path of the dangerous rays cast by the space fighter. Annoyed by Sparky's antics, the Quadrasone pilot maneuvered the craft and attempted a strike against the canine. The rays missed by a large margin, harmlessly hitting the restless waves of the bay.

The moon provided ample light for the retriever, for he could easily spot two fins in the water: his past adversary, 'Old Blue,' and another great white shark, bobbing in and out of the water in their favorite hunting spot. Sparky torpedoed down to the water.

The fighter closed in on Sparky, halting just inches from the water. The pilot hesitated before firing, and that was a mistake. "Dinner time," snickered Sparky.

Out from the depths breached two great whites, who each grabbed hold of the spacecraft, and dragged it into the water with them. The pilot and his ship were never seen again. One day, a lucky scientist would discover an alien spaceship lying at the bottom of the San Francisco Bay.

"Smooth sailing!" shouted Sparky. "Now, where is alien number two?" Just then Sparky heard a flurry of small explosions and sirens in the distance. He scoped the scene. A second fighter pilot began levying a barrage of laser rays on the pyramid-shaped financial services skyscraper. Folks streamed out of their houses; guests ran out of their hotels and restaurants.

Sparky zoomed over, spotting a flagpole that was jutting out from the side of a building. The retriever easily snapped the pole off and lodged it between his jaws. He drew closer to the enemy ship, about twenty yards away. With all his might, Sparky hurled the projectile toward the ship, but he missed the mark, and the flagpole crashed into another building, shattering several windows. Now the fighter knew he was there, and Sparky was in clear firing range. "Uh oh. This could be the end for me," breathed Sparky. There was no time to hide.

The pilot reached to fire his guns. Sparky squeezed his eyes shut. Then, out of nowhere, the enemy ship was rocked by a bolting beam of energy. It slipped and spiraled uncontrollably and crashed into an orange ball of fire against an office building. Sparky exhaled with relief and looked around incredulously to find who had saved his life. In the night sky, barely lit by the city lights and the remnants of the earlier destruction, sat Coladeus in a fighter jet of his own, grinning and giving a thumbs up. The smiling Trianthian headed over to his friend. The plexi-style window opened and Coladeus adjusted his language device. "How do you like our new toy? I wanted to be the first one to try it out."

Sparky shook his head in disbelief. "Where did you get this bodacious body of technology?"

Coladeus grinned. "It's been in the works. Since you and Elt saved me, I figured I return the favor."

A crowd had gathered below. Even a television van had stopped at the scene.

"We better split, Boss," advised Sparky.

"Precisely," agreed Coladeus.

The flying dog and the alien spacecraft flashed out of sight and hovered over a nearby park. Coladeus updated Sparky on the Quadrasonian invasion in Spring Valley.

"Well let's go help my buddy Elt!" charged Sparky.

"I'm afraid we have a situation to sort out first," explained Coladeus. "Follow me."

Minutes later, Army helicopters and Air Force jets from nearby installations arrived in the city, responding to all the distress calls. Debris from the crash site would be collected over the next few days, but there would be no proof of flying dogs or alien spaceships, for pictures from cell phones were too grainy and television crews hadn't arrived in time to capture any images.

Coladeus landed his vessel momentarily in the field behind Sparky's house, and Sparky landed right beside him. Amy was still standing in her backyard, dazed and confused. Sparky ran up to his human. She knelt down to hug him. When she gazed upward, all she saw was a short greenish creature walking towards her....

CHAPTER 33

ELT HAD THWARTED BANK ROBBERS, helped rescue time travelers, and aided in rejuvenating a dying planet, but facing an enemy like the Quadrasones was quite possibly the super dog's most challenging endeavor. One blast from the deadly ray from the Quadrasonian ship would surely end it all. The three ships branched out in different directions, one headed straight for Elt. If the pilot had possessed a mouth, he would have grinned, for Elt was in excellent firing range. Elt's only advantage was the night, for the combination of darkness and distance could cause an error, a mistake that would save the super dog's life.

In the blink of an eye, Elt devised a plan. The pilot fired. The laser headed straight for the canine, but Elt zoomed downward, like a high-diver careening off a diving board. The laser missed. The pilot geared up for a second strike.

Elt never stopped. He quickly turned upward, and lunged for the ship's underside, like a dolphin spiking a shark's belly with its snout. Elt pierced the vessel, rocking it backwards and out of control. Before the startled pilot could recover, Elt snatched hold of the craft's wing, swung the fighter round and round, and then released it. The ship soared over Main Street and crashed somewhere in the Spring Valley Park. Deputy Taylor witnessed the scene, but he couldn't detect Elt, for it was dark. To the deputy, it appeared as if the alien spaceship had spun out of control all on its own.

Elt dashed over in the direction of the second ship, which seemed to be heading toward his neighborhood…the Valleydale subdivision. In the distance, Elt heard another explosion, possibly in the direction of the observatory. Elt concentrated on his next challenge. Whatever that noise was, he would get to it. He had to protect his humans.

The super dog buzzed past the elementary school and caught up to the ship on Valleydale Drive. The Quadrasonian vessel struck its first target: Mr. Davis's shed, the place where the neighborhood pets used to hold their meetings.

"Get me out of here!" shrieked Sarge as he leaped onto his porch and scratched frantically at his back door. Through his window, Mr. Davis gasped in horror at the sight of his burning, smoking shed. He quickly opened the door to allow his Boxer to enter.

Ralph stared out his living room window. "What was that?" snapped Mr. Eltison.

"Not sure," responded Ralph. "Looks like an explosion!"

"I'll go out, you stay inside!" shouted Mr. Eltison running for the door. Ralph knew that Elt was somewhere out there battling whomever, and oh how he wanted to join his canine in another exciting adventure!

Prince begged Mr. Dawkins to let him outside. Prince's human resisted, for he didn't want anything to happen to his fabulous showdog. Finally, after endless yelps and scratches on the door, Mr. Dawkins conceded and opened the door.

Meanwhile, Elt whizzed in front of the ship and attempted to attract the Quadrasone's attention. He cut right onto Spring Drive. Rex's family had just awakened when they heard the commotion just down the street. Zach opened the door and released his German Shepherd to investigate the scene. Rex galloped all the way to his front fence and witnessed Elt's flight overhead. "Whoa," whispered Rex. "How can he do that? He seemed so…quiet." Rex referred to the times he had noticed Oleo. The replicate had avoided the German Shepherd at all costs.

If it worked once, it might work again, was what Elt was thinking. He attempted the same strategy as before, but this ship was too low, so Elt had to abort the mission. Elt now had to formulate another plan. His first goal was to lure the fighter out of his neighborhood, so the super dog crossed over into the jet's path and streamed back towards Valleydale Drive. Even though Elt's speed was an asset, the pointy-headed pilot remained aggressive and tailed Elt. A moment later, the enemy fighter pilot aimed carefully and fired.

The Quadrasone ray clipped Elt painfully on the right leg. He lost control in mid-air and landed in a heap in the bushes near Rex's yard. Slowly, but frantically, Elt struggled to extricate himself from the branches. He felt dazed and in pain but he knew he needed to escape. The pilot turned around and prepared to finish off his adversary.

Prince, who had jumped his fence and had raced down the street to investigate, noticed his friend in peril. He spotted Rex on the other side of the fence. "What are you staring at? Let's get him to safety!" Rex, who figured that this was no time to assert his pride into the situation, scaled his fence and joined the Doberman. Together they dragged the injured Elt to a safer place, under a row of bushes.

The enemy pilot relished his targets. He prepared to lay his final assault on all three of the canines. The pilot closed in and cackled in Quadrasonian glee as he aimed…

A gigantic thud slammed the space vehicle, and then another. The pointy-head, stunned by the impact, desperately searched the skies. Who had just attacked his ship? The attack continued as the left wing tore viciously off the spacecraft, and then the right. The engine was violently thrust out of its casing and heaved miles away. The pilot, along with the remnants of his ship, was catapulted miles away. A fiery ball erupted in the distance.

The fire from Sarge's shed lit the area well enough for Elt and his companions to see. Still dazed and wounded, Elt slithered his way from under the bushes. He saw two flying canines; one was a Labrador, presumably black and the other, a Collie. The two fliers nodded to the canines below.

"Your other flyer has been disposed of," related the Labrador. The two fliers zoomed off into the distance.

"Who in the heck was that?" asked Rex.

"Beats me," answered Prince. He turned to Elt. "Looks like you're not the only one who can fly." Prince had never met Sparky.

"Yeah, I feel like I know them," mumbled Elt. "Like I met them before." Elt stood up and began to shake off his confusion. Before he knew it, the effects of the ray had passed. "Thanks guys." Elt lunged forward, making sure his leg wouldn't give out on him.

"Where ya going?" wondered Rex. "We just witnessed some truly amazing things here!"

"Not as amazing as what I'm about to see," replied Elt. The super dog blazed past the Davis' house.

"Go. We'll secure things here," prided Prince. Rex nodded his head in agreement.

"I thought I was fast," commented Rex. "But these guys can jet."

Elt felt his strength recovering. He rocketed past the Greenlee house. Professor Greenlee was on the phone, standing on his front porch. He was too occupied talking on the phone to notice the mysterious Elt whizzing past him in a flash.

"I tell you there are aliens here in Spring Valley!" asserted the professor. "Yes, aliens!"

"Dad! Dad!" screamed Bryan. The boy stuck his head out of the front living room window. "Did you see the aliens? Trixie is really spooked again." Trixie's barking could be heard. Caroline opened the front door.

"Kids, get back inside and shut everything!" yelled Professor Greenlee. "It's dangerous out here!"

Back at the Eltisons', Ralph joined his dad outside. Together they cautiously walked down the street. Chin was still barking. They could even hear Old Max belting out a few grumps from inside Mrs. Petrie's house.

"Do you see him?" asked Mr. Eltison.

"No, but I think I know where he might be," responded Ralph. Ralph and his dad watched the Davis's shed burn. A firetruck, its alarm blaring, stopped in front of them. Fire crews jumped out of the truck and began preparations to douse the fire. The boy and his father moved on over past the Greenlee's residence. The professor hung up the phone in disgust and entered his home. The last stop was Jenny's house.

"Are you sure?" questioned Mr. Eltison. "It's awfully late."

"Dad, I don't think anyone is sleeping in this neighborhood tonight," returned Ralph.

"I guess you're right," stated Ralph's dad. "Go ahead."

Ralph knocked on the side door. About ten seconds later, Jenny opened the door. She looked tired, but happy. "Come on in."

Jenny led Ralph and his dad into the laundry room. There they discovered Ms. Rodgers, Bernadette, Elt, Jasmine, and four newly born puppies. Elt stood beside Bernadette, who was lying comfortably inside of the box with her young. The super dog bent down and licked each pup on the top of its head. He then reached over and kissed Bernadette.

Because the light was dim, Ralph strained to get a better view of the puppies. Two were black, and the other two were reddish-brown. The siblings nestled in a fluffy row beside Bernadette's belly.

The night was a late one, for Ralph and his Dad stayed for about an hour. Mr. Eltison enjoyed a cup of coffee with Ms. Rodgers, while Ralph and Jenny watched the puppies for a short time, and then raided the refrigerator for a late night snack. Elt was allowed to stay the night.

It was a night filled with action and emotions for the super dog. First, a celebration for his first year of life, even though he didn't quite understand what all the hoopla was all about. Then there was the battle with the Quadrasones. And who were the two new heroes that saved Elt's life? Where did they come from? Why did he feel like he knew them already? Last, he had become a father! There would be plenty of time for reflection later. Elt's job now was to be by Bernadette's side.

None of the super dogs knew it, but the battles were not over. The last battle, however, wouldn't be happening in Spring Valley.

CHAPTER 34

"WE'VE LOST CONTACT WITH BOTH of our squadrons," transmitted Dresant to his commander.

Zemak heard the news, but only had one thought on his mind. "Are we closing in on their ship?"

"Yes sir, but do we want our presence known?" questioned the first officer.

"By now they know we're here," returned the leader. "He knows we're here."

"Sir, we still have no confirmation that Coladeus is alive," Dresant reminded him. "We all witnessed him left for dead."

Zemak stood, his demeanor fiery and erratic. "He's alive, and their ship is reborn! Somehow, some way. Now it's time to finish them for good."

"But our shields are not fully operational," pleaded the first officer.

"Full speed ahead," commanded Zemak. He wouldn't hear any contradictions; he was determined to defeat Coladeus.

Dresant directed the helmsman to forge ahead at their highest velocity. Within a short period of time, through the use of advanced imagery, Dresant was able to pinpoint Trianthius I's exact coordinates. The Quadrasonian ship moved in.

Zemak's patience had worn thin. Dresant admired his commander, but feared that he was acting too hastily, especially with the weakness in the shields. They had previously paralyzed Trianthius I with their secret weapon, but they hadn't finished it off, for there it was in front of them...Trianthius I, fully operational.

The Trianthian vessel maintained its course, like no danger was in sight. The enemy ship closed in...closer and closer.

"Fire at once!" shrieked Zemak.

The directive was followed. The laser struck Trianthius I, but surprisingly, the ship remained unscathed, its defense system intact and formidable.

"Fire again!" demanded the leader.

The result was the same. The Trianthian shields were unaffected by the previously successful rays.

"This is impossible!" blasted Zemak. "Again!"

On board Trianthius I, Coladeus had just returned from his piloting mission on Earth. He was now seated in his captain's chair. "It's delightful to see that Mogulus's adjustments were favorable."

"Yes Captain," replied Matheun. "Shall we begin commencement procedures?"

Coladeus nodded. "Yes, commence please."

Trianthius I turned sharply in order to face the Quadrasone warship. The Trianthian spacecraft leveled a barrage of litoses rays upon Zemak's previously untouchable ship. With a weakened defense system, the Quadrasones had no chance. The damages were immediate and severe, causing chemical fires and explosions on both the interior and exterior of the vessel.

The warship limped away slowly in retreat. Zemak's angst and anger was a key ingredient to his defeat, for he rushed to judgement without considering that the Trianthians might have developed a remedy to their deadly ray. Would they get away? Would the warship make the trip back to wherever the Quadrasones originated from?

"Shall we pursue them, Sir?" asked Matheun.

Coladeus watched on screen as the enemy ship slowly faded away into the distance. "As you know, Trianthians are not an aggressive species. Although we have every right to destroy this race of beings for their actions, it is not our decision to do so."

Matheun paused momentarily. "Understood. Do we need to visit Elt before we go?"

"No, something tells me that all is well in Elt's world right now. I trust our agents assisted him?"

Matheun smiled. "Affirmative. Do you think Elt knows?"

Coladeus also smiled. "One day he will. What's our next mission?"

Matheun studied his scanner. "Readings indicate that there is a severe drought on the fifth planet in the next solar system."

"Off we go then," directed Coladeus. "I will take a rest in my quarters." Coladeus stepped over to the bridge elevator.

Trianthius I soared to its next destination. The Quadrasone threat had been eliminated. Earth and Trianthius were safe for now. It was possible that Coladeus would have to face Zemak once again. For now, the chances that the Quadrasones would survive were minimal.

CHAPTER 35

"THEY'RE SO CUTE, HUH?" INQUIRED Jenny as she picked up one of the black pups and placed him back behind the baby gate. The puppies had learned already how to scale the small barrier, ready to explore the rest of the Rodgers's living areas.

"I can't decide which one is my favorite," replied Ralph. "Is that one Cooper?"

"Yes, the black one with the white spot on his chest," affirmed Jenny. Jenny held another puppy, one that resembled Bernadette, up to her chest. "And this is Shelby. She looks like Bernie the most."

"And the one with a little brown mixed in with the red is Lucy?" guessed Ralph.

"And the other black one is the second boy…Pepper," returned Jenny.

"How did you come up with all the names again?" quizzed Ralph.

"They all were pet names Mom had when she was a kid," surmised Jenny. "I thought that was pretty cool."

Bernadette and Elt sat together in the living room while their children rolled around on the floor, jumping on each other and playing with Elt's favorite red ball.

"You think your dad is going to let you keep Cooper?" asked Jenny.

"I hope so," answered Ralph. "Perhaps Cooper will be my birthday present."

"Mom says we can keep one," announced Jenny. "I'm leaning towards Shelby right now. Bryan and Caroline are going to ask about Lucy. That leaves us with only Pepper to find a home."

Ralph reached over and rubbed Cooper's belly. He didn't possess Elt's exact markings, but the white spot on his chest, along with his black shiny coat, more or less was living proof that Elt was his father.

Bernadette's puppies had already made an impact on the families that lived on Valleydale Road. Besides Ralph, Caroline, and Bryan, all of the neighbors visited the Rodgers's house in order to catch a glimpse of the newest members of the family. Mrs. Yao praised the young ones for their playfulness, while Mr. Davis thought that they reminded him of Sarge when he was younger.

There would quite possibly be three additional canines to the neighborhood meeting one day if the Eltison and Greenlee families welcomed a new pup home. Even Zach Miller stopped by one afternoon to check out the new kids on the block. Ms. Rodgers attempted to persuade Zach to ask his parents about adopting Pepper, but Zach said that Rex was enough to handle already.

Elt and Bernadette had truly grown up fast, for they were puppies themselves just one year ago. Now they were the parents, and had to watch their children's adventures inside and outside the Rodgers's home. Their lives would definitely change. Elt would raise his son Cooper while Bernadette would attend to her daughter Shelby.

There would still be walks for the kids and their pets. The puppies were too young to venture out on the streets just yet. The walks allowed Bernadette time to exercise, breathe some fresh air, and enjoy the company of her human.

"She only put on a few pounds," smirked Trixie to Seymour later that day when the two were alone.

All in all, Trixie was quite excited to welcome the little tyke Lucy into the Greenlee family. It was time for her to be a mom in a way; nurturing and teaching a young one the ways of being a Greenlee.

Then there was the newest canine friend in the neighborhood... Rex. He learned first hand the secret talents of the dog that lived down the street. Never in his life would he have believed that one of his very own could fly, but he had witnessed the experience with his very own eyes. In fact, he saw *three* pooches soar in the air. Soon there would be a neighborhood pet meeting. Rex would meet Sarge, Chin, Juan, and Max. He already held the distinct pleasure of meeting the mighty Doberman, Prince.

Across the country, in San Francisco, one enemy ship rested on the bottom of the San Francisco Bay. The other ship was blown to smithereens, but scientists would find something of interest; alien DNA or a sample of a strange alloy not from Earth. There were, however, no sightings of a flying canine, just an unknown late night visit from a Trianthian to a twelve year-old young lady and her retriever.

In Spring Valley, the mysterious heroes that rescued Elt also took care of that third Quadrasonian ship that was headed in the direction of the observatory. Elt heard that explosion as he was soaring towards the Valleydale subdivision.

After Professor Greenlee's phone call to the authorities, there were visits from the military, scientists, and UFO officianados who wanted to discover some type of alien tidbit lying around. The professor had pictures from his telescope as proof, but only eyewitness accounts from folks in the city, as well as Deputy Taylor, described what they really saw...some type of unidentified spacecraft flying out of control and exploding. Could it have been fragments of an asteroid cast down to Earth?

Professors Van Hausen and Greenlee spearheaded an investigation, in coordination with authorities, which discovered little to nothing. The park was scoured; only burned pieces of a strange metal were detected. There was no sign of a pilot in any of the three supposed crash sites. Mayor Helms assured the town citizens that he would have the buildings repaired as soon as possible. The Towne Bakery and the Public

Library were hit the hardest. Businesses like Buttersample's, White's, Feldman's, and the Palace Theatre were spared any damage.

The insurance adjustor visited Mr. Davis's house and examined the destruction of the tool shed. Sarge sniffed the charred area as the adjustor snooped closely to see if any tool was spared during the explosion. There was no explanation for the shed's demise.

"So where do you want to go for your birthday dinner?" asked Ralph's dad.

"Probably Brown's again," answered Ralph.

"Do you want a party this year?" returned Mr. Eltison.

Ralph shook his head, no. "Elt's party was good enough. Is it still okay to keep Cooper?"

Ralph's dad sighed, and then smiled. "We'll see. How about we catch a flick after dinner?"

Ralph's smile gleamed. "That would be awesome, Dad."

Ralph didn't realize that Elt had almost met his fate on two different occasions; once onboard Klecktonis's ship, and second, just down the street from where they resided. All he knew now was that his dog was home and safe. He knew there would be more adventures, but hoped there would be a break in the action for a time. The boy looked forward to some quality time with his pooch, along with a possible addition to the family.

Elt watched his humans step inside the truck and drive off. He knew that they would return. He wasn't quite sure how long they would be gone, but if they didn't come back right away, Elt figured he could trek over to Bernadette's while he took care of business. Under the weeping willow, Elt thought he saw a small flash of light in the bushes ahead. It made the super dog reflect about the one little firefly that saved the Trianthian race. What would have happened if the insect hadn't stowed away on the alien's ship?

There was no way a lightning bug was still alive in October, but there was one, in a scientist's lab on Trianthius. Elt returned inside and found a comfy spot on the couch for a brief rest.

It had been a busy summer for the wonder dog. Hopefully fall would enable him to enjoy his family, both human and canine…

CHAPTER 36

IT WAS HALLOWEEN IN BORDERTOWN, late and thickly dark. The city's lights were barely visible due to a combination of fog and the smog from the nearby factories. The mansion was dark, except for a lone light upstairs. A sedan drove up to the front entrance. The gate opened, and the vehicle entered the grounds.

Hearing someone enter downstairs, the butler, Whitmore, grabbed his flashlight, exited his room, and cautiously stepped down the main stairwell.

"Who is that down there?" questioned Whitmore. The butler shined the light on the three men's faces.

"Get that light out of my face you fool!" demanded one of the men.

Whitmore dropped the flashlight in complete horror and disbelief. "Mr. Crum, I…I didn't know…"

The first man, Sid, opened the door to the study on the main level. He was followed by a man carrying a suitcase and wearing a mysterious black trench coat.

Crum watched the two men walk into the study. "Get a fire started Whitmore. It's going to be a long night."

"Yes, yes Mr. Crum," returned the butler.

Crum walked into the study and closed the door.....

ABOUT THE AUTHOR

Dan was born and raised in Newport News, VA. He attended Virginia Polytechnic Institute and State University. He has devoted nearly thirty years to the motion picture exhibition industry. Dan is currently employed with Lowe's Home Improvement.

Dan has enjoyed writing all of his life. He has written numerous screenplays, one which was pitched to a major movie studio in 2003.

When the author was ten, he wrote a story dedicated to his childhood canine Trixie. Years later, that story inspired him to create "The Adventures of ELT The Super Dog.Trouble on Trianthius is Dan's third novel in the "ELT The Super Dog" series.

Dan now resides in Frederick, MD. He and his three sons enjoy the company of their two dogs and five cats.

Printed in the United States
By Bookmasters